EMMANUEL SULLIVAN s.a.

Things old and new

An ecumenical reflection on the theology of John Henry Newman

Foreword by
Dr Mary Tanner

ST PAULS

St Pauls
Middlegreen, Slough SL3 6BT, United Kingdom
Moyglare Road, Maynooth, Co. Kildare, Ireland

© St Pauls 1993

ISBN 085439 438 9

Printed by The Guernsey Press Co. Ltd, Guernsey, C.I.
Produce of the EEC

St Pauls is an activity of the priests and brothers of the Society of St Paul who proclaim the Gospel through the media of social communication

Contents

In memory
of
Herbert Ward Keldany
[1907 – 1988]
Priest – Ecumenist – Friend of Newman

Foreword

The year in which we celebrated the centenary of John Henry Newman saw the production of many articles and books re-assessing the importance of Newman's life and work. Emmanuel Sullivan's description of his own tribute in *Things Old and New* is that it is 'no more than a modest essay'. It is in fact much more than that. At a time when some feel the ecumenical movement has stopped moving, Emmanuel Sullivan shows how Newman's thought can point us towards a radical renewal of Church life and a new spirit for the contemporary ecumenical movement. In particular he shows in a clear and convincing way how three characteristic elements in Newman's thinking about the Tradition of the Church, the development of doctrine and the need to consult the faithful can be keys to understanding contemporary puzzles on the ecumenical agenda. What he writes about receiving the fruits of ecumenical dialogue in the life of our Churches and about the approach to the question of the ordination of women is helpful and healing without closing either question one way or another. Emmanuel Sullivan helps us to think about both in the mind and the spirit of Newman.

The book is enlightening in its analyses of Newman's thought. But its great contribution lies in the insight it gives to the ecumenical pilgrimage in the last decade of this century. If these ecumenical lessons drawn from Newman's writings can be learnt we shall continue together, Anglicans and Roman

Catholics, within the wider ecumenical movement towards the visible unity of the one, holy, catholic and
apostolic Church.

Mary Tanner
December 1992

Introduction

'O Beauty, ever ancient, ever new, late have I loved thee' lamented Augustine of Hippo in his well-publicized confession. Christianity places love at its centre. It does so not because of some elusive internal spiritual experience of a nebulous higher power. It does so because of faith in a unique revelation of God's inner life and the tremendous generosity with which God shares that life with us through the presence of Jesus Christ in time and history. This Incarnation which Scripture describes as 'God in Christ reconciling the world to himself' (2 Cor 5:19) is the source of Christian faith and life. This is a faith in which God's love for all people is profoundly personalised for each one in his or her human condition and situation. Moreover, those who accept Christ are linked to God through, with and in him. They are called to share his ministry of reconciling love and form a community of faith in service to the human community. This community is the Church. Thus while the love of God is real, so also is our love and devotion for the Church. The Church is both an object of faith and a subject of faith, something running through our lives and engaging them in proportion to our faith. The Church is not an expendable element of our faith and devotion towards God. Nor do we think of it as an accident of history. It is the place where we begin our shared life with God in Christ. The Church's historical and temporal character creates a sense of tradition and development. The Church has a past and a future. It has a past because of

11

the original revelation given in Christ. It has a future because it has a prophetic role to proclaim the coming kingdom of God. Consequently while it is a guardian of revelation, it has to live in openness to the future. The Church expresses its identity in the light of all this as *one, holy, catholic, and apostolic.*

As a faith community Christians articulate their beliefs in human concepts and language. A theology of Church develops around the four marks of the Church – one, holy, catholic, apostolic. In the course of the centuries differences have arisen over what it means to be one, holy, catholic and apostolic. These differences have divided Christians. As time has passed such differences have kept Christians separated and identified by denominations which mark differences. Some of these differences are accidents of history and culture and the politics of a given time. Others are in fact doctrinal and are a matter of serious conscientious conviction on all sides of the divisions. Certainly denominationalism has marked the life of the Christian Church and impaired its inner life and prophetic witness in the world.

We live in a time when there is a significant movement to reunite the Christian Churches in one community of faith. This movement is called *ecumenical* and our age is often called an ecumenical age. The ecumenical movement takes into account all that has separated Christians. Its primary concern however is to discern through dialogue and co-operation those areas of doctrinal consensus as well as doctrinal differences. Ecumenism also tries to indicate areas where lesser differences – those accidents of history and culture, the malpractice of Churches, the misperceptions and suspicions we inherit – contribute to our continuing separation.

Still, ecumenism is not simply a matter of reconstructing visible unity among the Churches. There are issues which force themselves on the agendas of many denominations. Christians often share concern over such issues. Some issues become very divisive within denominations and Christians find themselves crossing the denominational divide in common concern over social and moral issues. The very urgency of such concerns brings us together and helps us work together even now for the future we believe God calls us to share through the Holy Spirit. This openness to the future stems from what is called the *eschatological* nature of the Church. This is a way of saying that the Church is called to point out the way on which humankind can find its way to God. The Church cannot look backwards all the time. Its prophetic and eschatological vocation compels it to look forward in response to 'the upward call of God in Christ Jesus' (Phil 3:12-16).

In our own time we work for Christian unity primarily by trying to integrate essential elements for the Church's life of faith despite differences, apparent or real. While this is the work of professional theologians, it is also the task of church leaders and other members of the Churches. This book is not the work of a professional theologian. Its intention is to persuade all members of the Christian Churches, especially those called upon to address and articulate ecumenical issues, to work towards a clearer understanding of what constitutes authentic church tradition. This entails the necessity of dealing with the legitimate development of church teaching and practice. A deeper awareness of the prophetic vocation of the Church is needed to energize contemporary Christians and open up the future to which God calls all people. I would like to persuade theologians, church leaders and active ecumenists to take advantage of seeds already sown in the Church. We need such Christians 'trained for the kingdom of heaven' like the scribe or faithful steward who knows how to bring 'out of his treasure what is new and what is old' (Mt 13:52).

In the last century there was such a man. If there is such a 'patron saint' for such an undertaking, it must surely be John Henry Newman. Through his work on Tradition, on the prophetical office of the Church, and the development of doctrine, all this combined with his spirit of openness to the Church's future, he opened the way for us to bring together the past and future of the Church in our time. His Victorian style may make him seem dated. His methodology which utilizes history, philosophy and theology; his apologetical and at times polemical lines of reasoning make him a complex, even convoluted subject. But if we remember that he was working within the context of the ecclesiastical scene of his day, we can reinterpret that context for our day and grasp that he was working towards an integration of key elements for the Church's life. The Church is beginning to acknowledge its debt to him. It is said that his spirit overshadowed and penetrated the Second Vatican Council. Ecumenists know what that Council meant for the movement for Christian unity.

It seems right to do more than remember the man and his work. At a time when some theologians and ecumenists ask whether Roman Catholics have 'received' Vatican II it is time to reflect on the foundation for church renewal laid by Newman. At a time when ecumenists ask whether the Churches are 'receiving' the fruits of ecumenical dialogue and the spirit of ecumenism it is time to go back to Newman. When the role of women in the life and ministry of the

14

Churches becomes an obstacle in the movement towards Church unity and a cause of anguish and disharmony in the Churches, it is time to address such an issue in the generous spirit of Newman.

This book claims to be no more than a modest essay, suggesting that if we look at Newman again we may find our way into a more radical renewal of church life and a new spirit for the ecumenical movement. We may gather courage from him to face both difficulties and doubts which generate new Church dividing positions. I have tried to write this tribute to John Henry Newman in his spirit, an eirenic spirit, which must become the new spirit of a new age. This new spirit has added a new dimension to Church life. It is characterised and expresses itself in *dialogue*. Newman's sense of the importance of dialogue finds expression at the end of one of his University Sermons (§10) preached in 1839. In this particular sermon he was dealing with those who supposed faith and reason to be irreconcilable. The words themselves could serve to describe how Christians in divided Churches understand and enter into dialogue as a first indispensable step which begins the journey to a rediscovered oneness in Christ and renewed church unity. With this in mind the words of Newman have a relevant ring for ecumenists:

Half the controversies in the world are verbal ones; and could they be brought to a plain issue, they would be brought to a prompt termination. Parties engaged in them would then perceive, either that in substance they agreed together, or that their difference was one of first principles. This is the great object to be aimed at in the present age, though confessedly a very arduous one. We need not dispute, we need not prove – we need but define. At all events, let us, if we can, do this first of all; and then see who are left for us to dispute with, what is left to prove. Controversy, at least in this age, does not lie between the hosts of heaven, Michael and his Angels on the one side, and the powers of evil on the other; but it is a sort of night battle, where each fights for himself, and friend and foe stand together. When men understand what each other mean, they see, for the most part, that controversy is either superfluous or hopeless.

Chapter 1

The Tradition of the Church

Tradition has a very general meaning. It can mean a lot of things. It may mean the acquired wisdom of a given community with its insights and skills which are passed on from generation to generation. New experiences are evaluated by the wisdom and past experience of the group. Tradition gives identity and dignity to any social grouping. It creates stability and community. It strengthens the structure of authority which uphold the tradition derived from past history. But it also has meaning for the future of societies inasmuch as it ensures a measure of organic development and provides a sense of direction for the future. This is a very general description of tradition. It is not to be confused with *traditions* or customs which have a symbolic function. These are arbitrary external modes of behaviour which serve to express *the tradition* of a community as we described it. While traditions or customs are subject to change, even to the point of becoming obsolete, essential tradition continues to conserve essential values, even though subject to developmental change. And within this general meaning of tradition it can come to be understood as *traditional ways* of thinking and acting. Or it can signify a reaction to new developments in the social group, a closure to new experiences. It could signify a reaction to what others perceive as a new level of awareness or consciousness which serves to open up the future.

When we come to speak of tradition or *the Tradition* in reference to the Church, we have to strive for a much more refined understanding of how we must use the word with its meaning. In this context, Tradition is the essential content derived from the oral teaching of Jesus and his immediate disciples. Later this teaching was canonized, so to speak, in written accounts or Scripture which was judged normative for the Church to receive, transmit and develop Christ's teaching faithfully and uniquely subject to the power and inspiration of the Holy Spirit. For this reason some Christian Churches view Tradition and Scripture, not as two sources of revelation, but together as one source – unwritten and written. This source is the Holy Spirit revealing something essential of the inner life of God and the divine economy for our world. Some Christian Churches have paid less attention to earlier oral tradition and the context in which the Scriptures were composed. Such forms of Protestantism have declared that Scripture *alone* is the only reliable source of Christian doctrine and belief. More recently some rapprochement between Scripture and Tradition has developed in the Churches. In the Second Vatican Council the Roman Catholic Church further refined its understanding in this matter, pointing out the close connection, indeed the conjunction of Scripture and Tradition, having one source and the same purpose. Needless to say, the Catholic and Orthodox Churches perceive themselves, each in its own way, as the bearers of this Tradition in the most complete sense and fullest measure. This sense of bearing Tradition has distinguished Protestant and Catholic in Western Christendom.

In the 1830's John Henry Newman was very much absorbed in finding a middle way or *via media* between Roman Catholicism and Protestantism. In his

18

Lectures on the Prophetical Office of the Church he reflects the tension felt in articulating the relationship between Tradition and Scripture.[1] At this time Newman is very ambivalent towards the value of Tradition. He seems to equate Tradition with a 'uniform custom', i.e. belief and action as Christians have always believed and acted. At the theoretical level he finds this a consistent explanation, but at the practical level it does not explain denominational peculiarities, especially when Roman Catholics are taken into account. He offers his own definition of Tradition. It is the Church's 'unconscious habit of opinion and feeling; which she reflects upon, masters and expresses, according to the emergency'. Steeped as he was in both classical and ecclesiastical antiquity it was natural for Newman to argue from the authority of antiquity in religious questions. For him it was a valid line of argument which took into account a time *before* the Christian Churches became divided. Much of our contemporary ecumenical dialogue employs this method of looking for a measure of consensus prior to the historic divisions among Christians. But for Newman this was the main kind of Tradition open to the Churches. At this stage of his intellectual pilgrimage he concludes that 'the Catholic Church, being no longer one in the fullest sense, does not enjoy her predicted privileges in the fullest sense'. Because of its ecclesial divisions the Church's purity of doctrine has been tarnished. And whereas the creed of Roman Catholicism 'is ever subject to increase; ours is fixed once for all'.

Here Newman, intent on avoiding a slippery slope, put his foot into a theological quagmire. He had to face the difficulty of creeds and articles of faith in the Churches. These creeds and articles enunciate and further articulate, and doxologically proclaim the essen-

19

tials of Christian faith. They do not necessarily list what Newman called 'the essentials of the Gospel'. He admits the difficulty he is in and has recourse to speaking of greater truths and lesser truths. Vatican II will speak of a 'hierarchy of truths', but this must not be confused with Newman's use of greater or lesser truths. Yet there is something of a foreshadowing here. He consigns the question of listing essential gospel truths to the question of what is necessary for the individual Christian. He says that such essential truths necessary for individual faith is not a matter for theology 'for theology is ever concerned with doctrines, abstract truths, not with their application'. He falls back on the Creed as symbol and rule of faith. Speaking of the Creed he says:

> Would the Fathers so have called it, had it not been the substance and centre, the measure and analysis of the whole counsel of God, so that nothing could be added really, because there was nothing to add *but what bore and depended upon it?*'[2]

To explain additions to the Creed or variations on it such as the Nicene or Apostles versions he simply says that these additions are words – not doctrines. Reading these *Lectures on the Prophetical Office of the Church* we sense the discomfort of Newman with this position. He is forced to admit that 'it may be urged then, that at least the Creed does not contain the rudiments of the whole revealed truth, even though it contains all its main elements...' In order to safeguard the primacy of the Creed, Newman makes a distinction between what he calls *Episcopal Tradition* and *Prophetic Tradition*. Episcopal Tradition is primary inasmuch as it 'is a collection of definite articles set apart from the first, passing from hand to hand, rehearsed and confessed at baptism, committed and received from bishop to bishop, forced upon the attention of each Christian and demanding and securing due explanation of its meaning'. Prophetic Tradition is secondary, i.e. second to the regulating teaching role of apostles and bishops. Newman recognized the role of prophets in the early Church and associates them with the later Doctors of the Church comparable to the association of apostles and bishops. Thus he says:

Apostles rule and preach, prophets expound. Prophets or doctors are the interpreters of the revelation; they unfold and define its mysteries, they illuminate its documents, they harmonize its contents, they apply its promises. Their teaching is a vast system not to be comprised in a few sentences, not to be embodied in one code or treatise, but consisting of a certain body of Truth, permeating the Church like an atmosphere, irregular in its shape from its very profusion and exuberance; at times separable only in idea from Episcopal Tradition, yet at times melting away into legend and fable; partly written, partly unwritten, partly the interpretation, partly the supplement of Scripture, partly preserved in intellectual expressions, partly latent in the spirit and temper of Christians; poured to and fro in closets and upon housetops, in liturgies, in controversial works, in obscure fragments, in sermons. This I call the Prophetic Tradition, existing primarily in the bosom of the Church itself, and recorded in such measure as Providence has determined in the writings of eminent men.[3]

21

Later I shall want to return to this distinction of the two traditions, suggesting that the Churches more seriously take into account the prophetic tradition. For now it suffices to note that Newman considered it a 'very different kind from the Episcopal Tradition, yet in its origin... equally apostolical, and equally claims our zealous maintenance'.

Though Newman extricated himself ingenuously from the quagmire I mentioned, the difficult task remained to relate Scripture as a record of Christian faith to Tradition as a living witness further expressing and articulating the true faith. Here, as a proponent of Anglicanism's *via media* or middle way, he criticizes Roman Catholicism for separating Scripture and Tradition as two distinct sources in matters of faith. He equally criticizes Protestantism for drawing on Scripture without the witness of Tradition. In the Anglican scheme for a 'rule of faith' Scripture and Tradition properly belong together. He says that 'Scripture is interpreted by Tradition, Tradition verified by Scripture; Tradition gives form to the doctrine, Scripture gives life; Tradition teaches, Scripture proves'. He concludes: 'Scripture when illuminated by the "Catholic religion", or the Catholic religion when fortified by Scripture, may either of them be called Gospel committed to the Church, dispensed to the individual.'

Prior to the publication of the *Lectures on the Prophetical Office of the Church* in 1837 Newman had entered into a controversial exchange of letters with a French Roman Catholic, Abbé Jager. This exchange went on from 1834 to 1836. This has received scholarly comment with actual texts by Louis Allen.[4] The controversy concentrated on the relationship of Scripture and Tradition. However, as Louis Allen comments in his Introduction, 'the notion of a developing

22

agency is obviously contained in this idea of a prophetical tradition'. It is important to remember that Newman in his long intellectual journey of faith had to move out of the sacred groves of antiquity into the ongoing life of the Church, through the centuries up to his own time. This is an important factor in Christian consciousness. The Church must be as concerned to respond to its future as it is concerned for continuity with and conservation of its past with its revelatory origins. The personal spiritual-intellectual maturation development of John Henry Newman is an example for our times as we move towards the future with an uneven pace. He strove to provide a solid theological base for the Church in his major works, *The Development of Doctrine*. This was first published in 1845 and revised in 1878.

In the Jager-Newman controversy Newman was pushed to reflect further on Tradition. In his first letter to Jager he said: 'Nor do we say that the proof of even fundamental doctrines must rest immediately on Scripture, but ultimately.' He went on to illustrate this by pointing out that the three orders of ministry were received as a discipline from Tradition. The baptism conducted by heretics is acceptable in terms of Tradition as a matter of doctrine that is non-fundamental, whereas we receive the doctrine of the Trinity as a fundamental doctrine immediately from Tradition, ultimately from Scripture. For him fundamental doctrines were those necessary for Church unity or communion. To receive what is a matter of discipline (orders), or what is non-fundamental (heretical baptism) is a matter of piety – not of necessity. Consequently he further distinguished what he called *pure tradition* (we might say with a small 't') from 'tradition based on and interpretive of Scripture' (we might say with a large 'T'). In his first letter to Jager he said: 'The reception of pure tradition is pious, of doctrines conveyed to us by Tradition but proved by Scripture is imperative.' In his second letter to Jager he made it clear that he 'did not find fault with the Council (Trent) for having established dogmas on Tradition alone, but for having made them fundamental articles, and insisting on their reception as necessary to be in communion with the Church'. He saw an essential difference between one who does not receive or subscribe to a certain truth and one who teaches a completely opposed doctrine, viz. a heresy. In this second letter to Jager he returns to his distinction between the Apostolical (Episcopal) Tradition and the Prophetical Tradition. The former 'is pure and worthy of faith' while the latter 'may have been corrupted in its details'. In his letter he gives a hint of that principle of the development of doctrine which would be one of his most significant contributions to Christian theology. In reference to the power of the Church he describes it as 'the power to develop its fundamental Creed into Articles of religion, according to times and circumstances; to develop is not to create'. With his third letter to Abbé Jager Newman returns to Scripture as the sole test of doctrine. However, this is not the classical Protestant claim for Scripture as the 'rule of faith'. Early in the letter he makes three notes by way of explanation:

1. Scripture is not to be contemplated by itself and deductions made from it without reference to Tradition;

2. Tradition is as much necessary to explain Scripture as Scripture is necessary to verify and circumscribe Tradition;

24

3. Scripture has the prerogative of being the document of final appeal in controversies and is ever to be honoured singularly as the formal and authoritative basis of teaching a tradition. As a matter of fact God has limited the revelation of doctrine to written documents and Tradition is limited to these except in accidental instances such as might happen in missionary preaching in the course of converting non-Christians to Scripture.

So, while we see the constrictions placed on the relationship between Scripture and Tradition, we can likewise detect Newman's efforts to establish a definite relationship between the two sources of Christian teaching. This tension in the relationship of the two sources continues to be problematical in Protestant-Catholic dialogue. Biblical renewal in the Roman Catholic Church and the theology of Vatican II's Constitution on Divine Revelation have gone a long way towards relieving the tension. This document did not explicitly describe Scripture and Tradition as separate sources but affirmed 'a close connection and communication between them' (c. 2, no. 9).[5] Inasmuch as both Scripture and Tradition are related to the teaching of Jesus and the ongoing inspiration and activity of the Holy Spirit the Vatican document indicates a certain unity between them. At this stage of his thinking Newman could not be expected to achieve such understanding. He was limited by his view that the authority of antiquity was valid only before the historic divisions in the Church. There is no ongoing magisterial office. The office of bishop is limited to holding and teaching the Creed in the Episcopal Tradition. The Prophetic Tradition is too diffuse, even subject to some measure of corruption. Pure tradition which deals with

25

doctrines not found in Scripture or Tradition but based on fundamentals found in Scripture and interpretive of Scripture will not suffice either. Pure tradition remains a matter of pious belief, a matter of counsel rather than precept. Limited as it was, Tradition at this stage of Newman's thought was basically conservative with an eye to the past and to history. Only later, particularly in his study of the Arian and Monophysite heresies would he begin to understand the ongoing nature of Tradition with a teaching voice of authority in continuity with the past while oriented to the future. This was to lead him eventually to Roman Catholicism.[6] Here and now we are interested in the future of the Church in the last decade of the second millennium. If we are to value Tradition, we must be prepared to give it a future as well as a past. Tradition is a process. While Newman may not be immediately helpful, his attempt to work with Scripture and Tradition encourages us to deal with what is still an unfinished piece of ecumenical business. Perhaps if we look more closely at his notion of the Church's prophetic role we will find a balance for Tradition in its function of conserving and continuing the past as the Church moves towards its own fulfillment in God's kingdom.

Tradition and prophecy. These belong together. Apart from Tradition, prophecy becomes visionary, the function of seers and fortune-tellers or doomsayers who foretell a future in precise terms and imagery. It becomes the haunt of fundamentalists. In fact prophecy is closely related to teaching and Tradition. This is why Newman related the prophets and Doctors of the Church in his understanding of Prophetical Tradition. The Nicene Creed confesses belief in the Holy Spirit who has spoken by the prophets. Prophecy is one of the principal charisms of the early Church. Paul lists it

26

second to apostles and prior to teachers (1 Cor 12:28). In Ephesians 2:20 the prophets are associated with the apostles as the foundation of the Church. They are associated with teachers of the Church who hand on and interpret the faith. By their proclamation, inspired by the Spirit, they prepare a way for the Church to discern the present and move into the future. They enable the Church to move eschatologically from what already is to what is not yet. A charism is a gift of grace endowed by the Spirit on individuals for the common good of the Church. The Church is fundamentally charismatic as a Spirit-led community. This is not often taken into account when we discuss theological 'models of the Church.'[7] If we run through the various charisms listed in the Pauline epistles, it is evident they are listed not simply in the order of importance, but to point out their mutual interdependence ensuring a fundamental charismatic ordering of the Church (1 Cor 12:4-13). This charismatic dimension has to be associated with whichever model we use when speaking of the Church. Vatican II renewed and reminded the Church of its charismatic character in its Constitution on the Church known as *Lumen Gentium* (c. 2, no. 12). When we think of the ecumenical movement over the last twenty-five or thirty years in the mainline Churches. It has been a confessing Church in this respect, confessing the ongoing acitivity of the Holy Spirit as acknowledged in the Nicene Creed as 'the Lord and giver of life'.

In the course of the Church's history this practical awareness of the charismatic dimension of Church life shifted to the institutional dimension. It can be argued that this was a loss to the Church even if institutionalism is defended as necessary to curb excessive and erroneous enthusiastic movements. Hans Küng in his work

27

The Church illustrates such shifts at different periods of Church history.[8] But he adds that such misleading enthusiasm and false charism ought not be countered by negative opposition which all too often inflicts the Church with needless divisions and the proliferation of sects. There must be constant reference to how authentic charisms build up the Church as a community of the Lord's disciples witnessing to unitive love and peace poured out by the Holy Spirit. In this way the Church becomes credible in its witness to the gospel of reconciliation preached by Jesus and committed to the Church. In the same work Küng makes another point which seems important for what I am suggesting, viz. that we take the future dimension of Tradition more seriously than heretofore. He suggests that we avoid an 'exaggerated concentration on the *apostolic succession*' and remember that there is also a *succession of prophets and teachers* – to say nothing of other charisms'.[9] This point deserves serious reflection. At any rate we may well echo the question he raises in *The Church*: What becomes of a Church in which the prophets and teachers are silent? It is not my purpose here to enter into a discussion of the relationship of the theologian to the Church's teaching office. Several charisms can co-exist in the individual including official teachers in the Church. We are not justified in excluding teachers of theology or those holding an authoritative position in the Church from the reception of other charisms. The interpenetration of charisms is a reality. Excessive institutionalization of charisms fossilizes or desiccates what is meant to nourish Christian life and witness. In the charismatic renewal movement it is often said regarding the gifts of the Spirit: 'Use them or lose them!'

A serious obstacle in this matter of relating proph-

ecy to Tradition lies in thinking of prophecy as anti-
quarian, a gift meant for the early Church, but now
obsolete since the Church put in place its institutional
structures, ensuring proper discipline, order, and dignity. They may also mistakenly be associated with a
kind of fundamentalism. In the 1970's the charismatic
renewal movement faced such objections from many
who were and remain suspicious and fearful, even
hostile to this renewal movement. Yet the renewal of
this dimension of Christian life was part and parcel of
early Christian life, a permanent building block of
Church life. As noted, Ephesians 2:20 speaks of the
Church being 'built upon the foundation of the apostles and prophets'. To both are committed the task of
preaching the word of God. It is not a matter of the
extraordinary nor a matter of ecstasy, of visions or
voices. It is teaching and proclaiming that Christ Jesus
is the cornerstone of the Church. Nor are prophets free
agents wandering about on their own, opining and
proclaiming on every situation in the Church. In the
early Church they did not have the same power as the
apostles and were subject to apostolic authority. Küng
says:

> The apostle is an original witness and messenger
> who has authority vis à vis the community... The
> prophet on the other hand is subject to the authority
> of the apostle. He has authority *in* the community,
> as a member of the community in communion with
> the other prophets who have the same authority...
> He is limited by the original apostolic witness... in
> agreement with the faith laid down by the apostle.
> While the community is not in a position to judge
> the apostle, it has the right and duty of discerning
> between spirits... And... the whole community re-

mains responsible for testing the genuineness of spirits... The role of prophecy is the edification of the community by words of encouragement and consolation, by the preaching of repentance and of promise...'[10]

If Tradition is ongoing and essential for the life of the Church; if it is not simply and solely a reference to Scripture, chapter and verse, then prophetic succession ought to enjoy a kind of succession, as Küng suggests, as an authentic component of Tradition in order for it to remain vital, credible, appealing to the future as well as the past. Christianity is rightly concerned about its doctrinal moorings in the past. It has been called, however, to announce the 'newness of life' in the Risen Christ (Rom 6:4). It is about the future as much as it is about the past. You cannot hand on without 'handling' that which you wish to pass on. Tradition does not remain untouched, unchanged in any way, antiseptically passed from generation to generation. Change in this sense is development which seeks fullness of faith – faith not only in the richness and beauty of God's revelation in Christ, but faith seeking how it may best respond to what God asks and where the Holy Spirit leads in our time. What is the Spirit saying to the Churches? This is always a fair and pertinent question.

This brings us back to John Henry Newman. He lived his life in this prophetic mold. He was doing much more than reflecting on his own personal journey of faith. He was thinking of Tradition when he spoke of the development of doctrine and said:

In time it enters upon strange territory; points of controversy alter their bearing; parties rise and fall around it; dangers and hopes appear in new relations; and old principles reappear under new forms. It changes with them in order to remain the same. In a higher world it is otherwise, but here below to live is to change, and to be perfect is to have changed often.'[11]

The invitation is extended to all to accompany Newman on his pilgrimage of mind and spirit. Now in midlife (1845), he completed his *Essay on the Development of Doctrine*. Ian Ker notes in his biography of Newman that the *Essay* was his public farewell to the Church of England. In October of the same year he entered into full communion with the Roman Catholic Church. What is important for us in this ecumenical age is to respect such transitions and look for the gifts we bring to one another. In the *Essay on the Development of Doctrine* we find a significant ecumenical clues for our future unity. We cannot live in our past exclusively. All our traditions have a past out of which we move presently towards a future which discloses itself if we move in faith. All our traditions must be faithful to *the Tradition* of the undivided Church.

NOTES

1. The text is from the Parker edition of 1837.
2. *Lectures on the Prophetical Office of the Church*, Parker ed. p. 266. Italics mine.
3. Ibid. p. 296.
4. Louis Allen, *John Henry Newman and the Abbé Jager*, Oxford University Press, 1975.
5. References to the documents of Vatican II are taken from the Abbott edition unless otherwise noted.
6. Cf Ian Ker, *John Henry Newman: A Biography*, Oxford: Clarendon Press, 1988. This work has been described as a biography which gives a

31

reasonably full personal life of Newman and also serves as an intellectual and literary biography. Ker relates the growing unease of Newman with the notion of the *via media*. He quotes him as saying that as an integral system it has 'never had existence except on paper...' (pp. 139-144).

7. Cf Avery Dulles, *Models of the Church*, Dublin: Gill & MacMillan, 1976. This is a well-known work with reference to various models of the Church, e.g. the Church as community, as institution, as sacrament, as servant, as herald of the Gospel.

8. Hans Küng, *The Church*, London: Burns & Oates, 1967, pp. 191-197.

9. Ibid. pp. 433 ff.

10. Ibid. p. 396.

11. Cf *The Development of Doctrine*, London: Longmans, Green & Co., 1906. This oft quoted passage can be found in Chapter 1, at the end of the first section of this edition. p. 40.

Chapter 2

The development of doctrine

Newman was neither naive nor unduly optimistic in articulating his philosophical theology of development. He was aware of the constant need for renewal in Church life. He speaks of 'real perversions and corruptions... often not so unlike externally to the doctrine from which they come, as are changes which are consistent with it and true developments'. And he is quick to add that 'corruption in religion is the refusal to follow the course of doctrine as it moves on, and an obstinacy in the notions of the past'.[1] It is important to note that in the preface to the later 1878 edition of the *Essay on the Development of Doctrine* he speaks of important alterations – not in its matter, but in the arrangements of its parts and in the text.

Newman's method entailed a philosophical approach to questions of theology and doctrine. For example, when he speaks of an idea we have to keep in mind that for him an idea was something living and real. It lives insofar as it is received by the mind. It is real insofar as it embodies a claim to be true. Thus Christianity is an idea which is real and living. An idea is not objective in the sense that it is one thing, one reality, or one fact grasped once and for all time. It is not simply one mind taking in an idea from its objective base on a one to one relationship of subject to object, a theory of knowledge. An idea in Newman's thought has a lot of complexity and a lot of interaction between what is known and who knows it. So he defines the *idea* as that which 'represents an object or supposed object' as 'commensurate with the sum total of its possible aspects, however they may vary in the separate consciousness of individuals; and in proportion to the variety of aspects under which it presents itself to various minds is its force and depth, and the argument for its reality'.[2] He says that there is 'no one aspect deep enough to exhaust the contents of a real idea, no one term or proposition which will serve to define it; though of course one representation of it is more just and exact than another, and though when an idea is very complex, it is allowable for the sake of convenience to consider its distinct aspects as if separate ideas'.[3] Christianity is such an idea and the real reason for his Essay on Development. It is the idea which above all grows gradually into a body of thought. Part of the process involving many minds is to bring the complex notion of Christianity into consistency and form. This phase of the development signifies 'the germination and maturation of some truth on a large mental field'. But to be authentic development all aspects of an idea assembled together 'constitute its ultimate shape' and really belong to the idea from which they start.[4] He makes the point that the development of an idea can be a matter of a longer or shorter period of time. And this development, e.g. Christianity, can be influenced or modified by the context in which it is lived or by the circumstances which surround it.

Another dimension of Newman's thought is the matter of truth and certitude. It was in the *Essay on the Development of Doctrine* where he used the language of finding evidence of truth. He speaks of a 'collection of weak evidences' which 'makes up a strong evidence'.[5] This method of proof which Newman uses as a very important part of his apologetical methodology is called a *convergence of probabilities*. For him the use of reason in the service of faith is not that of scholasticism. By that I mean it is not a straightforward deductive line of rigorous syllogistic reasoning. He used and refined the method of converging probabilities. To illustrate this method of reasoning he compared it to 'a cable which is made up of a number of separate threads, each feeble, yet together as sufficient as an iron rod'. He liked this mechanistic analogy because in mechanics 'all display is carefully avoided, and the weight is ingeniously thrown in a variety of directions, upon supports which are distinct from or independent of each other'.[6] As Ian Ker notes, by 1853 the term 'assent' had acquired a firm place in Newman's philosophical vocabulary. Assent follows proof by means of an act of the will. Reason says that a proposition *ought* to be believed and is presented to our free will which accepts or rejects it. Hence in religious matters faith is not a conclusion from premises. It is the result of an act of the will following a conviction that to believe is a duty. Assent does not admit of degrees nor does certainty. *Certainty is an assent of the intellect to assent as an act of the will.* His epistemology rests on proof out of a convergence of probabilities leading to assent which leads to certainty. For him this is the best explanation of how faith and reason relate. He refined this relationship through the years, particularly in his famous *Grammar of Assent* (1870). But for our purpose such basic understanding will suffice.

Much has been said and contested over how to interpret Newman's intellectual basis for his work on the development of doctrine. Was he thinking of de-

35

velopment in terms of how the mind and conscience of the individual develop? Was he thinking of the world in which he lived, influenced by the immediate context of life at Oxford? Or was he working out a larger vision of life and the human condition? Some have even suggested that his image of development was derived from his own personal development, an autobiographical paradigm. Others feel that the model of organic evolution – evolution in a straight line – provided the model for his work on development of doctrine. Such academic exchanges will undoubtedly go on. We are concerned here to remind the Churches that John Henry Newman's intellectual and spiritual pilgrimage hold valuable insights for the ecumenical movement. He wrestled with problems which are still with us. We saw something of this in the first chapter. However, with his notion of development he more directly offers valuable insights for ecumenical efforts to reconstitute the visible, credible unity of the Churches. However commonplace it is to speak of the scandal of a divided Christendom proclaiming a gospel of reconciliation, it is nonetheless truly scandalous. We need a way of doing theology together. Even more we need a perception of future church unity which is not a fantasy of returning to the past, to a supposed 'golden age' of Christian unity. Our perception ought to be one which enables us to envisage a richer unity than ever before, one born out of centuries in which the Holy Spirit continued to distribute gifts and graces despite schisms and heresies and the malpractices of separated Churches. As we come together we bring gifts and graces with us, enriching our new unity in Christ. Such a perception opens us to the ongoing work of the Holy Spirit. And this has practical value for ecumenists who are concerned about the

36

reluctance and hesitancy of the Churches to receive the ecumenical movement. It also enables us to work towards the resolution of Church dividing issues such as the ordination of women.

Elsewhere I have referred to the question of reception as a new factor in the ecumenical movement.[7] The unity of the Churches in their inner denominational life and in their relationships with one another very much depends on how we keep a spirit of reception alive. Here I understand 'reception' to mean a spirit of openness to receive the newness of life offered by the Spirit to the Churches. It also means fidelity to the Tradition of the Church through the ages. This might mean the non-reception of something proposed for the Churches to take into their system. For some Churches there is difficulty with episcopacy as it is theologically understood by other Churches. And we know how tentative the question of ordaining women to priesthood is felt to be in some Churches, nothing short of impossible in others. We need some legitimate flexibility in how we discern and understand Tradition. Nicholas Lash speaks of such in *Newman on Development*. He says: 'One of the factors that has contributed most powerfully to the striking convergence, in recent years, of Catholic and Protestant positions... has been the recovery of a far richer, more flexible, and more traditional concept of tradition.'[8] Lash, referring to Newman's *Essay on the Development of Doctrine*, says that it is 'permissible to recognize, in the *Essay*, the elements of a theology of tradition which has today proved acceptable' despite a notable residue of Church unity problems to be solved.[9] Elsewhere Lash notes one of the weaknesses of the *Essay* lies in 'its espousal of a concept of the *unity* of the Church which cannot acknowledge "ecclesial reality in any denomi-

37

nation other than the Roman Catholic Church".'[10]
Today, Lash notes, when we think of the development
of *all* Christianity, we cannot expect Newman 'to cast
much *direct* light' on our contemporary ecumenical
problems. Still, we have to remember that Newman
was dealing with the *idea* of Christianity as an instance of a living and real idea facing society at large,
viz. the meaning of the revelation and self-disclosure
of God in our history.[11] While Newman's light may be
indirect lighting it is essential because it is examining
the revelation underlying Church doctrine. Such examination remains an essential in the quest for Church
unity. Newman provides that 'large mental field' on
which to work through some of our ecumenical problems. Lash confirms this when he says: 'Any "theory"
of doctrinal development depends, in the last resort,
upon the conception of revelation that underlies it.'[12]
Revelation must be the common concern of Christians. It is not so odd then to turn to Newman for
whatever light his theory of the development of doctrine can throw on our common path to Christian
unity, the response of faith to what God has revealed
in Christ.

Before moving on to a reflection on the *Essay* itself
there is another problem. Stated simply it asks whether
Newman's theory is not his way of saying that development is really *continuing revelation*. Assuredly the
language of development is new and bears little re-
semblance to the language of the original revelation.
Since language derives from experience, it would seem
that either development is a new revelation of some
truth or completely divorced from revelation and hence
not doctrinal development at all. Newman would answer this difficulty by saying that in some sense there
are 'new doctrines', but they are part of the original

38

deposit of faith. Newman was clarifying this matter as late at 1868. Thanks to Stephen Dessain an unpublished paper by Newman written in 1868 confirms this sense of new doctrines which are nonetheless part of the original deposit of faith. He says that such doctrines are not simply deductions made by theologians who are able 'to reduce them to their relations to other doctrines, or give them a position in the general system of theology'. He says immediately: 'To such theologians they appear as deductions from the creed or formulized deposit, *but in truth are original parts of it*, communicated per modum unius to the apostles' minds, and brought to light in the minds of the Council, under the temporary illumination of Divine Grace.'[13] Earlier he had described such development as 'the germination and maturation of some truth, or apparent truth on a large mental field'. He would say that biblical revelation is based on the principle of development inasmuch as we have to interpret the prophecies and types of the Old Testament in the light of Christ. We give meaning, the meaning of *fulfillment* to the text and the type. Following on he would say that the utterances of Our Lord and the apostles are parallel to these earlier Old Testament prophecies which are also subject to development because they are to be fulfilled in Christ. Newman would say that the whole of Scripture is written on the principle of development. This of course rests on the analogy of how prophecy is fulfilled in both Old and New Testaments.

Lash criticizes this use of the analogy as having only limited value in proving later stages in the course of revelation. As he sees it, Newman never satisfactorily resolved the problem which would deny the character of continuing revelation to doctrines which have been developed later in the Church's history. More-

39

over it has left Newman open to misinterpretation in this matter of development and continuing revelation.[14] In his second letter to Abbé Jager, Newman is quite clear that the Church has 'the power to develop its fundamental Creed into Articles of *religion*, according to time and circumstance...'. However, he says that 'to develop is not to create'. From this it would seem that he did not identify development with a new revelation. Still, as Lash says: 'It is not difficult to see that the broad theological perspective within which Newman is operating is closer to the theology of revelation and tradition in *Dei Verbum* (the Vatican II Constitution on Divine Revelation) than it is to preconciliar neo-scholastic catholic theology.'[15]

So far in this chapter we have been clearing the ground of some of Newman's philosophical and theological presuppositions in order to take an honest look at his *Essay on the Development of Doctrine* which we will simply refer to as the *Essay*. We will look at the aim of the *Essay* and some general features of his thinking as we read through it.

First, the aim of the *Essay* is basically defensive in accord with his apologetical methodology. Positively he is concerned to present a new view of the relationship between contemporary Christianity and the Church of the early Fathers. He deals with this relationship specifically in terms of Roman Catholicism. Lash forewarns us in *Change in Focus* that 'those who read the *Essay* expecting to find a systematic and unified theory of doctrinal development, in the twentieth-century sense, either find what is not there, or else are disappointed'.[16] Lash points out that while today we may take development in Church doctrine, life, structure for granted, Newman could not. He had to work from the general fact of development to offer an hypothesis which would serve to demonstrate that change is part of life and not every change a corruption. 'He is here... arguing negatively; making out a persuasive apologetic case for the claim that the existing doctrine and practice of the Roman Church are not necessarily "corruptions".'[17] He also distinguished carefully development from an 'enlargement' of doctrine. For Newman, development has to be a 'harmony of the whole' which leaves the basic doctrine what it was all along. When we promulgate a new truth it must be a harmony with and cognate to the old truth implicit in it and related to it. In his *Apologia Pro Vita Sua* he applies this to the thorny problem of infallibility. He says: 'Infallibility cannot act outside of a definite circle of thought, and it must in all its decisions, or definitions... profess to be keeping within it... The new truth which is promulgated, if it is to be called new, must at least be homogenous, cognate, implicit, viewed relatively to the old truth.'[18] Infallibility then is about judgement and decision making; it is not inspiration, revelation or new information.

However necessary and valuable the argument from harmony and logical coherence (not logical deduction) another norm is necessary to distinguish a true development from a false development. A development may be formally logical but nonetheless a corruption of the original idea. There must be intelligibility and coherence. There must also be *external authority* which authenticates the development, keeping it in line with the tradition of the community. And there must be *reception* of this development as official teaching by the community as a whole. Newman was to write an article in 1859 *On Consulting the Faithful in Matters of Doctrine*. He revised it in 1871. I want to speak of the significance of this article in another chapter. For now it is important to remember what John Coulson says in his introduction to his edition of the article: 'This work is fundamental not only to a fuller understanding of Newman's theory of doctrinal development, but to an appreciation of the importance he attaches to the laity in his theology.'[19] More to our present point, Newman was relating the notions of *authority* and *reception* to supplement his concept of *coherence* and *harmony* as constitutive of true development. This enables us to see his own developed understanding of Tradition as constituted by Church authority and reception on the part of the faithful members of the Church as a whole. Yves Congar confirms this when he says that 'Newman... made a decisive contribution to the problem of the relationship between magisterium and history in tradition.' Congar prefaces this remark saying that Newman's idea of development 'became an inner dimension of that tradition'.[20] By his insistence that there be a normative principle, viz. Tradition, Newman was careful to distinguish true developments from false ones. Let us look at this more closely as his theory unfolds in the *Essay*.

General description: Newman considered particular developments taking place over a longer or shorter period of time. The time factor depends on how long an *idea* takes to be 'brought into consistency and form...' according to the time it takes to achieve that 'harmony of the whole' of which he speaks. He also envisages the development as taking place 'on a large mental field'. This means that development 'is carried on through and by means of communities of men and their leaders and guides...' (*Essay* 1.1.5).[21] Moreover, development must be 'like an investigation worked out on paper, in which each successive advance is a pure evolution from a foregoing [idea]' (1.1.5). When we apply development to theology ' 'the mind may be employed in developing the solemn ideas, which it has hitherto held implicitly and without subjecting them to its reflecting and reasoning powers' (1.2.9). Thus, 'if we turn our attention to the beginnings of Apostolic teaching... we shall find ourselves unable to fix an historical point at which the growth of doctrine ceased, and the rule of faith was once for all settled' (2.1.12). He concludes that 'Christian doctrine admits of formal, legitimate, and true developments... contemplated by its Divine Author' (2.2.17). He argues for the need of an infallible developing authority in matters of Christian doctrine. Since Christians are subject to bias, controversies arising from prejudices of birth, education, place, personal attachment and party politics, 'it can hardly be maintained that in matter of fact a true development carries with it always its own certainty even to the learned, or that history, past or present, is secure from the possibility of a variety of interpretations' (2.2.1).

It is worth noting that Newman returns to his earlier notion of a *prophetical tradition*, though 'from a very different point of view from that which I am taking at present'. He describes this tradition as 'that body of teaching... in various forms and measures of truth... partly being a comment, partly an addition upon the articles of the Creed' (2.2.2). From this position he continues to argue for a rule of faith 'necessary for arranging and authenticating these various expressions and results of Christian doctrine'. In Newman's thought the need for a rule of faith arises from the need to distinguish minor points of belief from major truths of faith. He speaks of 'greater and lesser truths', the former necessary to believe, the latter a matter of pious belief. He asks: 'How are we to discriminate the greater from the less, the true from the false?' (2.2.2). For him the answer lies in the doctrine of the infallibility of the Church by which he meant 'the power of deciding whether this, that, and a third, and any number of theological or ethical statements are true' (2.2.4). It is beyond our scope to pursue his argument for infallibility in detail which he does in the remainder of chapter two of the *Essay*. He devotes chapter three to the historical arguments on behalf of the development of doctrine using his method or proof from the 'convergence of probabilities', i.e. all the evidence taken together. He justified this by saying that 'the less exact methods of reasoning may do His work as well as the more perfect...' (3.2.2). Chapter four of the *Essay* consists in illustrations which substantiate the evidence for the development of doctrine which he describes as a movement from imperfect to ever growing evidence which delays the process while inferences and judgements are being made and reasons 'producible to account for the delay' (4.1.2). The second part of the *Essay* begins with chapter five in which he contrasts genuine developments with what he calls 'corruptions' of Christian faith. This chapter is the centerpiece of the *Essay* for it is here that he names seven tests or characteristics to distinguish true developments from corruptions. It is important to look at all seven in some detail. It may prove helpful to list them in their simple form:

1. preservation of type;
2. continuity of principles;
3. a unitive, assimilative power;
4. logical sequence in terms of faith – not reason by itself;

5. the feeling there is a future to be anticipated and the development is faithful to what has been anticipated;
6. development conserves antecedent developments as an addition which illustrates and corroborates the body of thought from which it proceeds;
7. duration, persistence, or the chronic vigour of what has been developed.

All seven notes are important in the development of an idea because through them the unity and identity of what is being developed can be ascertained and accounted as one and the same reality. Let us look at each one in greater detail.

The preservation of type. Here Newman uses an analogy borrowed from physical development, not unlike that used by Vincent of Lerins in the fifth century with reference to Christian doctrine. Newman quotes him: 'Let the soul's religion imitate the law of the body, which as years go on, develops indeed and opens out its due proportions, and yet remains identically what it was. Small are a baby's limbs, a youth's are larger, yet they are the same' (5.1.1). Later, in chapter six of the *Essay*, Newman will apply the preservation of type to contemporary Catholicism. He does this by way of an historical analysis of the Church in the first six centuries as it contended with various heresies such as the Donatist, the Nestorian, and the Monophysite. In treating this first note of development he says that 'one cause of corruption in religion is the refusal to follow the course of doctrine as it moves on, and an obstinacy in the notions of the past' (5.1.8).

Continuity of principles. Here he works analogically from mathematics. 'Doctrines stand to principles

45

as mathematical definitions to the axioms and postulates of mathematics' (5.2.1). Principles are abstract and general; doctrine deals with facts. Doctrines grow and are enlarged while principles remain permanent. For example, consideration for the poor is a doctrine of the Church. It is a principle when one considers the Church as a political power. Doctrines are developed by the operation of principles. If you are an Epicurean, belief in the transitory nature of the world leads to the doctrine of pleasure; if you are an ascetic, it leads to mortification. 'A development, to be faithful, must retain both the doctrine and the principle with which it started (5.2.3). When principles are lost, corruptions set in. 'Thus as to nations, when we talk of the spirit of a people being lost, we do not mean that this or that act has been committed... but that certain lines of thought or conduct by which it has grown great are abandoned' (5.2.6). In this way Newman makes a case for the continuity of principles assuring true development. It was natural for him to contrast the Reformation with Catholicism by way of illustration (7.1.4.7). He cites the continuity of Catholicism with the Incarnation in its ability to hold together faith, dogma, theology, sacraments, Scripture, grace, asceticism, sin and mortification (7.1.3-4). The Catholic Church holds all these principles together in continuity with the Incarnation, its central truth and principle.

The power of assimilation. Here the analogy is with the physical world whereby a particular life grows by taking into its system, into its very substance, some external material. In such a process two elements become one. He notes that this is sometimes an effort as in the case of feeding animals 'who lie torpid for a time under the contest between the foreign substance

46

and the assimilating power' (5.3.1). When this analogy is applied to the realm of ideas or doctrines he describes the process as first polemical, then seemingly eclectic, and finally unitive. As he says, 'a living idea becomes many, yet remains one' (5.3.2). Again he says: 'The stronger and more living is an idea, that is, the more powerful hold it exercises on the minds of men, the more able it is to dispense with safeguards, and trust to itself against the dangers of corruption' (5.3.5). The Church in its long history takes into its system many things good and bad. Its healthy constitution enables it to sort out chaff from wheat, what is dispensable from what is indispensable. Here again we have to keep in mind Newman's special reference to the Church of Rome which he says 'can consult expedience more freely than other bodies, as trusting to her living tradition...' (5.3.5).

Logical sequence. It is hardly necessary to say that when Newman refers to logic in the context of development he is not thinking of formal syllogistic logic whereby the mind progresses from one judgement to another until a rational conclusion is reached. Rather he is referring to a logic which grows out of the development of one's life. There is an original idea, e.g. Christianity. It remains in the mind, becomes familiar and distinct and colours all other relationships. As he says, 'a body of thought is gradually formed without his recognizing what is going on within him... And thus he is led to regard as consequence... what hitherto he has discerned by a moral perception and adapted on sympathy; and logic is brought in to arrange and inculcate what no science was employed in gaining' (5.4.1). It is only afterward that we see a true development, not as deterioration, error or confusion, but as something natural and harmonious. Perhaps an instance of such logical sequence can be found in the New Testament (Acts 10:47-48) where Peter, referring to the experience of the gentile Cornelius and his companions, says: 'Can anyone forbid water for baptizing these people who have received the Holy Spirit just as we have. And he commanded them to be baptized in the name of Jesus Christ.' This true development, a logical outcome of the original teaching, viz. incorporation into Christ is by water and the Holy Spirit. Such logical sequence involves faith and not only the logical use of reason.

Anticipation of a future. Newman continues to speak of an idea as *living*, i.e. influential and effective. It makes things happen. It assures development 'which is to come, though vague and isolated', and which 'may occur from the very first, though a lapse of time be necessary to bring them to perfection' (5.5.1). He uses an analogy from the history of great men who from childhood or boyhood displayed a penchant for what afterwards became history. Charmingly he says: 'The child Cyrus mimics a despot's power, and St Athanasius is elected bishop by his playfellows' (5.5.2). He applies this note to history extensively. In relation to Christian doctrine he refers the Incarnation and Resurrection to certain Catholic practices of venerating relics, the cult of Mary and the saints, the ideals of martyrdom and virginity. And accordingly he brings his erudition of early Church history in support of his position. Chapter ten of the *Essay* is devoted to some applications of this note – anticipation of a future.

Conservation of the past. 'A true development... may be described as one which is conservative of the course of antecedent developments being really those antecedents and something besides them: It is an addition which illustrates, not obscures, corroborates, not

48

corrects, the body of thought from which it proceeds...'
(5.6.1). His argument here is not that there be 'a strict
correspondence between the various members of a
development' which is 'more than we have a right to
expect'. He falls back on the analogy of human development. 'The bodily structure of a grown man is not
merely that of a magnified boy' for 'manhood is the
perfection of boyhood, adding something of its own,
yet keeping what it finds' (Introd., c. 11). He singles
out the Catholic practice of the sign of the cross as a
development directly related to the doctrine of the
Cross. Of course it also serves the doctrine of the
Trinity. He devotes a section of chapter eleven to
show that there is no real evidence that devotion to the
Blessed Virgin obscures the divine glory of her Son.
For all this he cites the Church's principle derived
from the Incarnation itself: *Non amittendo quod erat,
sed sumendo quod non erat*, i.e. the Word of God
became truly human not by ceasing to be what he was
(divine) but by assuming what he was not (human).
This note which is concerned with conserving the past
belongs in a special way to Christianity. He refers to it
as having the 'character of addition' which is a change
'real and perceptible, yet without loss or reversal of
what was before...' Rather such change is 'protective
and confirmative' of what went before (Introd., c. 11).

Chronic vigour. Newman says that corruption is
not longstanding, whereas true development endures
and stands the test of time. Such changes are persistent
while changes that corrupt are transitory (5.7.1). He
considers this a general law and in the final chapter of
the *Essay* applies the note of chronic vigour to Christianity. This is a living religion, an energetic religion. It
is progressive despite its detractors for 'it grows and is
not overgrown... spreads out, yet it is not enfeebled; it

49

is ever germinating, yet ever consistent with itself'
(1.2.2). I find this seventh characteristic of development most appealing. It is one of the easiest to grasp. It
is related to the religious phenomenon in general. It is
what Andrew Greeley called 'the persistence of religion'.[22] In the sixties and seventies there was a good
deal of talk about people coming of age, not needing
faith or a sense of the sacred. Some theologians talked
about the 'death of God'. The secular city was said to
be self-contained and sufficient. There is not so much
of this sort of talk about in the late eighties and as we
begin the final decade of the century.

In concluding this cursory review of the *Essay* it is
important to understand that there can be no simple
logical deduction from the seeds of thought and theory
provided by Newman. There is no way to draw rigid
demonstrable conclusions. This is especially so if we
expect these to be directly applicable to some of our
contemporary issues, two of which will form chapters
five and six of this book. However, his thought must
be reckoned an invaluable source for moving towards
the future of the Church's ongoing life.

Nicholas Lash suggests that 'a fresh examination of
Newman's *Essay on the Development of Doctrine* may
prove fruitful, since Newman was one of the first
Catholic theologians seriously to attempt to hold in
tension the demands of historical consciousness and
the Christian conviction that the Gospel of Jesus Christ
is irreplaceable and unchangeable'.[23] Lash, a theological scholar of Newman's *Essay*, is convinced that we
must not let Newman's own stress on the hypothetical
nature of his work and its failure to test exhaustively
the hypothesis against historical data derogate from its
contemporary theological value. Lash asks 'what light
can the *Essay* cast on the significantly different situa-

tion in which Christian theology today attempts to come to terms with the problem of change and continuity in Christian doctrine?'[24]

Thus far we have looked at Newman's efforts towards a more complete understanding of Christian Tradition. Further, we reflected on his apologetic for the development of Christian doctrine. There remains another dimension of his thought to be considered for our purpose. It is often said in ecumenical circles that we need to do theology together. By 'together' I would understand a wider need to reflect on our Christian faith together. This of course includes theologians, ecumenists, and church leaders. But it ought to include the whole Christian people who, as members of a community of faith, are called and set apart to declare the wonderful deeds of God who called us out of darkness into his marvellous light (1 Pet 2:9). This 'togetherness' is the widest extension of the *laos*, the whole people who make up the Church. The role of the *laity* is today an essential issue for the Churches together, though more pressing for some than for others. To approach other urgent issues of faith and order in Church life apart from the role of the laity would amount to an anorexia of faith and future for the Church. It often amounts to what John Coulson calls 'spiritual apartheid'. We go back to Newman who wrote about this and suffered for it. In 1859, when he wrote his article for *The Rambler*, he was asking for trouble. The article entitled: *On Consulting the Faithful in Matters of Doctrine* created an ecclesiastical minefield. Newman took the risk with his usual integrity and courage. It brought him suffering and misunderstanding and earned for him from one of his fellow clergy the designation of being 'the most dangerous man in England'.

NOTES

1. *The Development of Doctrine*, London: Longmans, Green & Co., 1906. Using this edition I refer to the *Essay* in the text according to chapter, section, and number, e.g. (5.1.8) with footnote references to the page numbers of this edition, pp. 176-177, for Newman the whole process of Christian Tradition was associated with his understanding of an 'idea' as having a life and a history.
2. Ibid. p. 34.
3. Ibid. p. 35.
4. Ibid. p. 38.
5. Ibid. p. 107.
6. As quoted in Ian Ker's *Biography*, op. cit., pp. 620-623.
7. Cf *Ecumenical Trends*, vol. 15, no. 7 (July-August 1986), pp. 105-110.
8. Nicholas Lash, *Newman On Development*, London: Sheed & Ward, 1975, p. 122.
9. Ibid.
10. Nicholas Lash, *Change in Focus*, London: Sheed & Ward, 1973, p. 91.
11. Ibid. pp. 91-92.
12. Ibid. p. 92.
13. Stephen Dessain provides the background for this hitherto unpublished paper in the *Journal of Theological Studies*, vol. 9 (1958), pp. 324-335.
14. *Change in Focus*, op. cit., pp. 92-95.
15. Ibid. p. 92. Revelation, Tradition, Magisterium are cognate terms connoting content, process, expression respectively.
16. Ibid. p. 88.
17. Ibid. p. 89.
18. *Apologia*, Oxford Edition, London: Henry Frowde, Oxford University Press, 1913, p. 345.
19. *On Consulting the Faithful in Matters of Doctrine*, ed. by John Coulson with an introduction, London: Geoffrey Chapman, 1961.
20. Yves Congar, *Tradition and Traditions*, London: Burns & Oates, 1966, pp. 209-211.
21. Because of frequent references to the *Essay* these are given in the text according to the 1906 edition of Longmans, Green & Co. following the divisions into chapter, section, number, e.g. (1.1.5).
22. Andrew Greeley, *The Persistence of Religion*, London: SCM Press, 1973. The introduction is well worth reading in relation to Newman's 'chronic vigour'.
23. Lash, *Newman on Development*, op. cit. pp. 1-2.
24. Ibid. p.4 .

Chapter 3

Consulting the faithful

As noted at the end of the last chapter, Newman gave us two versions of *On Consulting the Faithful in Matters of Doctrine*. The first article was written for *The Rambler*, a Catholic periodical, in 1859. He revised this controversial article in 1871. John Coulson has provided us with the two versions and a very helpful introduction by way of background for reading the two versions.[1] These articles deal with the process whereby any doctrine reaches the stage of a formal declaration and definition of the doctrine as a matter of faith for Roman Catholics. Part of this process involved asking what the belief of the whole Church is – lay and clerical. This requires discernment regarding the actual belief of the faithful as testimony that the doctrine under consideration belongs to the Apostolic Tradition. This consultation considers all the faithful as a 'body of evidence'. Therefore the laity are to be consulted since they are witnesses to the fact of revealed doctrine. Their consensus is a real and indispensable part of the voice of the infallible Church. It is important to be clear what Newman understands by such consultation. For the consensus obtained serves as an indicator or instrument by which the Church is infallible in such judgements of faith. According to Newman 'infallibility is *in* the *consensus fidelium*', but that 'consensus' is an *indicium* or *instrumentum* to us of the judgement of that Church which is infallible.[2]

Newman insisted that infallibility not be confused with the power and prerogative of the Church's teaching authority to define doctrines binding in faith, i.e. *de fide*. Equally, he wished to make clear that the assent of the laity is more than a notional or passive assent or an implied faith. It is a real assent of the mind and the heart. It is no accident that he chose the third edition of his work: *The Arians of the Fourth Century* (1871) to append the revision of his original *Rambler* article of 1859. It was during the Arian heresy against the divinity of Jesus that 'the governing body of the Church came short, and the governed were pre-eminent in faith, zeal, courage, and constancy'. He says that 'the Nicene dogma was maintained during the greater part of the fourth century, not by the unswerving firmness of the Holy See, councils, or bishops, but by the "*consensus fidelium*".' Far from wishing to divide the Church between its official teachers and the rest of the Church, Newman was concerned to show that the infallible teaching of the Church resides in the whole community of faith and not exclusively with its official teachers. He is not saying that the infallible party in the Church consults the fallible part in order to reach an infallible decision. Logically this would be nonsense and theologically absurd. John Coulson refers to a point made by Professor Chadwick that *Consulting the Faithful* was 'Newman's first attempt to resolve publicly one of the major difficulties in his theory of doctrinal development: how, before a definition, is the mind of the Church to be discovered?'[3] Coulson himself later makes a comment along a similar line:

The importance of *On Consulting the Faithful* is that it removes the argument from the realm of

54

policy and discipline, and places it firmly within the context of theology; it has ceased to be a series of charges and countercharges, of a dispute about the Bishop's behaviour over a particular question of educational co-operation, and has become an argument about the laity's place in the very heart, mind and structure of the Church.[4]

In arguing his case for a much more effective consultation of the laity Newman uses the definition of the Immaculate Conception of 1854 as an example. This definition of doctrine he describes as a *conspiratio*, a word implying unison, harmony, and a spirit of concord between official Church teaching and what was ready for reception on the part of the Catholic world. These two elements he said 'are put together, as one twofold testimony, illustrating each other and never to be divided'.[5] The distinction between a teaching Church and a learning, listening Church was part of the Catholic theological idiom prior to Vatican II (1962-1965).[6] This distinction is used with much greater nuance in today's Catholic theology. Both teachers and learners teach and are taught in various ways. There is a mutuality in the learning process between those who teach and those who are taught, between lay and cleric, bishop and priest, pastor and parishioner. This mutuality in the learning process ensures and makes more credible the *consensus fidelium*, for the faithful are all the members of the Church irrespective of office and function in the body of Christ. Hence, the distinction between a teaching Church and a learning Church can never add up to a separation of the hierarchy from the laity. Ian Ker, in his biography of Newman, mentions a remark he made in reference to his own Bishop Ullathorne to the effect that he 'has a terror of laymen, and I am sure they may be made in this day the strength of the Church'.[7] Monsignor Talbot, a staunch critic of Newman, described the role of the laity as one in which they are able 'to hunt, to shoot, to entertain' but definitely not 'to meddle with ecclesiastical matters' where 'they have no right at all...'[8] This gives us some idea of the situation in Newman's time, though probably not all that crudely put. When Newman was asked to establish a Catholic University in Ireland, it seemed doomed to failure because he wanted 'to make the laity a substantive power in the University'.[9]

What Coulson said bears repeating, viz. that while the conflict around Newman was in the context of his educational policy and the politics connected with this policy, the real issue was his theology of the laity; his insistence on the evidence that several points of faith have been determined and defined on the basis of a *consensus fidelium*. This expression is helpful if we remember that *consensus* is not a matter of *consent* as we commonly understand it. *Consensus* means an agreement in faith, an agreement that a certain teaching is a matter of faith. Such consent is rooted in a spiritual instinct, a spiritual sense for what is part of the deposit of faith, consonant with the apostolic faith. This is often referred to in its Latin form as the *sensus fidelium*, an instinct for true belief. The faithful are of course all members of the Church actively engaged in a life of faith, lived in the power of the Holy Spirit, with a consciousness of the Church's witness and mission in the world. As we have said, these matters of faith and belief always involve a measure of interaction and *consultation* between faithful members of the Church – lay and clerical. The contribution of John Henry Newman to this dimension of Church renewal proved invaluable in the course of Vatican II. This Council addressed the role of the laity and the spiritual instinct for faith, the *sensus fidelium*, which keeps the whole Church moving and growing and developing its faith and understanding of the great truths of creation and redemption.

The laity. One has only to refer to the indices of either the Abbott or Flannery editions of the official documents of Vatican II to see how extensively the role of the laity is treated. The Council issued a Decree on the Apostolate of the Laity on 18 November 1965. In the Abbott edition of the Decree by way of introduction, Martin Work speaks of the lay apostolate as simmering on the 'back burner' for nearly two thousand years. In this official statement of the Council it has been put on the 'front burner' and the heat turned up. Twenty-five years later it has certainly not reached 'boiling point'. In the same edition Cynthia Wedel commented to the effect that there had been a growing awareness in all the Churches that the Church's mission 'cannot possibly be carried out in the modern world unless the entire membership of the Church shares actively in that mission'. The laity do not play a secondary derivative role in the life of the Church. Yet, there is even now a tendency to assign and confine the role of the laity to temporal and secular affairs as the proper sphere of their activity and service to the Church. There is insufficient attention paid to their service and contribution to the internal life and affairs of the Church. While it is not the extreme position of a Monsignor Talbot, quoted earlier on, there is nonetheless a facile assignment of roles to laity, religious, and clergy which virtually separates rather than distinguishes the life, witness and service of laity, religious, and clergy. This ideal of lay involvement in the life of

57

the Church is yet to be realized. The Decree on the Laity and chapter four of the Constitution of the Church have gone a long way on paper. In actual practice in the post-conciliar Church there is a much longer way to go. Witness to Christ and service to the Church remains confined largely to temporalities or the application of talents to practical parish needs or public moral issues. There is more of a 'Catholic action' outlook than a *sensus fidelium* which directly affects the formation and development of Christian doctrine in faith and practice. In her comments on chapter three of the Decree on the Laity of Vatican II Cynthia Wedell says: 'A Protestant misses here a stronger emphasis on a share in the actual government of the Church. This may be an area where the Catholic Church will have to gradually make some changes' (Abbott ed.).

Sensus fidelium. Newman's wish to make the laity a 'substantive power' in the University was rooted in his vision of the Church. He was not charging that doctrines were defined without *any* reference to the actual faith of the laity – implicit or explicit. This was not the case in the definition of papal infallibility, the Immaculate Conception, and later, the Assumption. But difficulty arises in approaching an issue for which there seems to be or in fact is no precedent. In some cases there is no Tradition to look back to. Such for example would be the new principles of ecclesiology employed in dealing with the ecumenical movement or the possibility of the ordination of women. Both examples are discrete issues to be treated singly and separately. I use them because they are areas where the way ahead is far from clear, in fact is obscure and uncertain. As such we need a new sense of faith in all the faithful – lay and clerical. To try and reach a *sensus fidelium* without the laity is to come out with a malformed faith. Plainly speaking, church leaders need to trust the laity more. The Constitution on the Church (*Lumen Gentium*) is explicit:

> The body of the faithful *as a whole*... cannot err in matters of belief. Thanks to a supernatural sense of the faith which characterizes the people *as a whole*, it manifests this unerring quality when... it shows universal agreement in matters of faith and morals. For, by this *sense of faith* which is aroused and sustained by the Spirit of truth, God's people accepts not the word of men but the very Word of God. It clings without fail to the faith once delivered to the saints, *penetrates it more deeply by accurate insights, and applies it more thoroughly to life.*[10]

Lumen Gentium really means the Church as a whole. It quotes St Augustine for whom it meant 'from the bishops down to the last member of the laity'. The Abbott edition mentions this as a 'favourite theme of Cardinal Newman, who foresaw its importance for the theology of the laity, which was in its infancy in his day'. And the Flannery edition of the same passage makes a note that *sensus fidei* in the text 'refers to the instinctive sensitivity and discrimination which the members of the Church possess in matters of faith'. To sum up, this crucial element in the Church's life of faith we might say that it is an instinct for true faith in all the faithful by the grace of the Holy Spirit (*sensus fidei in omnibus fidelibus in Spiritu*). If there is a feeling of disappointment that the Council did not elaborate more on this faith element, it does indeed function in the conciliar documents as a real dimension of the Church's official teaching.

Finally, it is necessary to keep in mind that this developed instinct for the faith in theory and practice is a constituent for the development of doctrine. Again it is worth reflecting on a very important passage from Vatican II's Constitution on Divine Revelation:

This tradition which comes from the apostles develops in the Church with the help of the Holy Spirit. For there is a growth in the understanding of the realities and the words which have been handed down. This happens through the contemplation and study made by believers who treasure these things in their hearts (cf Lk 2:19,51), through the intimate understanding of spiritual things they experience and through the preaching of those who have received through episcopal succession the gift of truth. For, as the centuries succeed one another, the Church constantly moves forward towards the fullness of divine truth until the words of God reach their complete fulfillment in her.[11]

Here is a statement which views Tradition in relation to the development of doctrine. Once more one wishes that the Council had been more explicit and expansive about this relationship between Tradition and the development of doctrine. However, the Constitution focused on another vital relationship, viz. that of Scripture and Tradition. Yet, the relationship between Tradition and development is no less important. It takes the weight and stress off Tradition as that which deals with the past and puts it in equilibrium with the future, the eschatological dimension of the Church's life. To say this is not to suggest that Tradition deals with the future in any facile way. Nor does it seek its confirmation simply by looking back into its own Church history. Both are a matter of contemplation and community reflection over long periods of time. Congar reminded us of a University Sermon preached by Newman in 1843 in which he portrays the Mother of Christ as the model in this respect. Significantly Newman used the references to Luke 2:19,51 as did Vatican II.[12] The sermon on these texts was in fact entitled: *The Theory of Developments in Religious Doctrine.* Congar treats Tradition as history and development – not simply as *transmission*. He says: 'Thus Tradition is development as well as transmission. It is impossible that the religious relationship of men with God should be preserved without its substance bearing fruit. That which was received and professed in baptism becomes in the context of Christian life, praise, service, witness, response and decision.'[13]

Congar notes that while Tradition is a preservative, it is not something dead and unproductive because it is 'lived and defended, generation after generation' of Christians. The deposit of faith can be grasped only 'within that living communion whose richness can only be partially expressed at the level of explicit understanding'.[14] Consequently the development of doctrine cannot be justified in terms of developments in history or secular consciousness. These must come from within the Christian community. This is a vital principle when we come to speak of controversial issues in Church life such as the ordination of women as priests. While this does not cover our present ecumenical situation of divided Churches acting unilaterally, the principle is valid for the praxis of any Church. Congar says: 'Mere history can go no further than the purely human phenomena in which the fact of Christianity is expressed. It cannot read it as the Church does because it has not her insight.[15] This brings us back to the *sensus fidei* and the *sensus fidelium*. Congar describes this sense of faith in the faithful as 'a faculty for grasping the implications, as not yet elucidated, of a reality which is already *in its possession*'.[16] This is in no way a diminishment of the historical dimension of Church life, certainly not of history itself. Congar, turning to Maurice Blondel's view of Tradition as development, says that 'there takes place a constant interchange between primitive historical facts and faith, by which interchange Christian awareness gathers precision.' In this sense 'Tradition does not make an addition: it is definitely not a mere repetition of the primitive fact or its statement.'[17]

Eschatology. Tradition and development, then, are in no way mutually exclusive. Rather they are intimately related. The point of a living Tradition is not to justify doctrinal development but to give it direction towards the fullness of life and truth promised in the Gospel. It is a process involving all members of the Church and affirming our faith in the Holy Spirit's presence and activity throughout the Church. This process raises Christian consciousness as a community of faith and not just another institution. If the Church were just another institution, its processes would be purely historical and its role as a prophetic of the kingdom of God hold little meaning. But it is both a community of faith and prophetic institution living in the heart of the world, concerned about human affairs. Its task is to provide continuity between past and future. In *Visible Unity and Tradition* Max Thurian observes: 'The Church is progressing towards the Kingdom not only in its concrete life but also in the increasingly rich understanding it receives of the Word of God.'[18] The reception of God's word needs the active response of the laity as well as the hierarchy. Their mutual interaction is necessary for the Church to hone its sense of fidelity to the prophetic task of announcing and preparing the way for the coming kingdom of God.

Summary. In these three chapters we have reflected on three elements of John Henry Newman's religious thought: the Church's Tradition, the development of Church doctrine, and the need to consult all the faithful in matters of doctrine. We have seen to some degree how interrelated these elements are – not only in the thought of Newman but for theology itself if it is to serve the believing community to articulate and communicate the Christian mystery of faith relevant to the human condition and situation. In each age the Church is on a pilgrimage of faith. Ours is no exception. In fact we Christians share in the world's transitions. In our time we live in a shrinking world with expanding technology on a fragile planet. In this world the Church has to exhibit stability and mobility. To use a phrase of Teilhard de Chardin, it has to be 'a pilgrim of the future on its way back from a journey made entirely in the past'. It has to be like the faithful scribe mentioned in Matthew 13:52 'who has been trained for the kingdom of heaven' and 'is like a householder who brings out of his treasure what is new and what is old.' The Church needs tradition, development, and wholesome community life for all its members. It has need for internal cohesion and vibrant witness. It needs a renewed unity which respects diversity. For it lives in an ecumencial age where the search for this unity is bedevilled by a history of divisions which have damaged its credibility. The Churches are wounded with suspicion of one another's intentions, with recrimination and mutual misrepresentation. We now have to speak of the Church and the Churches, not in the older sense of a communion of Churches but in the sense of an imperfect communion which keeps us separated in doctrine and worship. It is not only the credibility of the Church which has suffered. It is the witness to Christ and his mission in the world that has suffered. Then there are new moral issues, new social-political realities which overlap with problems facing the rest of the world. These are often divisive within Church denominations.

In chapters five and six I address two such Church dividing issues. These affect directly the future life of the Churches in their search for Christian unity. These are the reception of the ecumenical movement into the ordinary life of the Churches, i.e. as a dimension of church life as opposed to optional peripheral isolated ecumenical activities, and, secondly, a dispassionate reflection on the question of the ordination of women to presbyteral and episcopal ministries. What we have been doing in examining some of the thoughts of John Henry Newman is to look for seminal principles and a context for further reflection on these two issues which will profoundly condition the future progress of the ecumenical movement and that of Christian unity itself.

Yet, we cannot simply 'leap' from Newman's theology as reflected and developed in these three areas, viz. Tradition, the development of doctrine, and the sense of faith in all the faithful people of the Church, to an immediate application of his theology to such contemporary theological problems. This would be neither honest nor valid. Some bridging is necessary – not to pass over a chasm or abyss of theological differences, but to allow Churches to continue their common pilgrimage in a new time with its own concurring difficulties towards the goal of Christian unity. The next chapter suggests some materials gathered from John Henry Newman to help erect such a bridge.

NOTES

1. *On Consulting the Faithful in Matters of Doctrine*, op. cit. in note §19 of chapter 2.
2. Ibid. p. 67.
3. Ibid. pp. 26-27.
4. Ibid. p. 36.
5. Ibid. p. 71.
6. This distinction is expressed in the Latin terminology of the *ecclesia docens* and the *ecclesia discens*.
7. Ian Ker, *John Henry Newman: A Biography*, op. cit., p. 363.
8. Cf Coulson's introduction, op. cit., p. 41.
9. Cf Ker, cit. supra, pp. 408, 481-9, 494, 566.
10. Abbott edition, n. 12; cf footnote 40.
11. *Constitution on Divine Revelation*, Abbott ed., n.8.
12. Yves Congar, *Tradition And Traditions*, op. cit., note 20 of chapter 2, pp. 253-270.
13. Ibid. p. 266.
14. Ibid. p. 269.
15. Ibid. p. 219.
16. Ibid. p. 318; cf pp. 319-321, 327.
17. Ibid. p. 366.
18. Max Thurian, *Visible Unity and Tradition*, London: Darton, Longman & Todd, 1964, pp. 121-122.

Chapter 4

Newman – Bridge for
a pilgrim people

A book review in the *Church Times* (14 September 1990) was headlined: 'Cardinal Newman's Significance Today'.[1] David Newsome, the reviewer, felt 'the very exercise of looking for relevance [in Newman] is practically meaningless when one considers the extent to which the world has changed over the last hundred years in its attitudes and priorities (and above all its fulfillment of Newman's prophecies on the march of infidelity and secularisation)'. We hardly need to be reminded that the Church has changed as well as the world in the course of these hundred years. The Church, however, claims to be more than a human institution entirely subject to the vagaries of time and the human condition. It is an instrument, a sign and a mystery of God working within time and the human condition. As such the Church is subject to change. As mystery it is tied to the revelation of God in Christ. And as such presents to us 'an admirable consistency and unity in word and deed, as her general characteristic, but crossed and discredited now and then by apparent anomalies which need, and which claim, at our hands an exercise of faith'.[2]

Newman's *Essay on the Development of Docrine* which we have looked at previously provided a way of testing later doctrinal positions as to their correspondence to the original deposit of Christian revelation. In

67

other words, were these later expressions of doctrine true to the original idea of Christianity? Francis Davis says of the *Essay on Development*: 'It was not aimed at proving that later dogmas were developments of earlier ones, or even of the statements of the Scripture text.'[3] Another way Newman might have expressed his aim in writing the *Essay* is posed by Davis in the form of a question: 'Does the Church in all its expressed teaching and practice of today show itself to be essentially the same as the Church at the beginning, or at any period of its history?'[4] This was really what Newman had in mind when he gave us his famous seven notes or tests to distinguish true developments from corruptions in doctrine and praxis in chapter five of the *Essay on Development*. He wanted to witness to the identity, the consistency, the historical continuity of the living word of God entrusted to the Church through the ages.[5] Newman trusted the Church's basic instinct for true faith. This was not a blind or naive trust. He grounded it in the Church's history and its infallible ability to reach the truth eventually in any situation compatible with its life and mission. But he was careful not to confuse such infallibility with impeccability, ever aware that the Church does not always practice what it preaches. Precisely for these reasons Newman's theology is remarkable for its openness.

Newman's theology was open to development, unafraid of new ideas and practices, based as it was on a profound trust in the Church as holy, as the Body and Bride of Christ, a divine institution, 'the shrine and organ of the Paraclete, who speaks through her till the end comes'(Preface of 1877 to the Lectures on the Prophetical Office). Quoting an Anglican poet in the same place, he describes the Church as '"His very self below" as far as men on earth are equal to the discharge and fulfillment of high offices, which primarily and supremely are His.' Newman was prepared intellectually and spirtually to bring out of the Church's treasure things old and new. Can we doubt that he would not have been caught unaware of the ecclesiogical developments of the Second Vatican Council in the course of which the Roman Catholic Church officially committed itself to the ecumenical movement? Most certainly he would have seen that the real though imperfect communion with other Churches espoused by his Church to be an instance of a post-Reformation development rooted in an older conception of the Church as a communion of Churches, diverse but united. He would have seen clearly the aim of such a movement – full visible communion in faith, sacramental life and mission. In such controversial matters and practice such as the ordination of women to presbyteral and episcopal offices it is not stretching things too far to suppose that he would see the issue as a legitimate theological question whichever side of the issue succeeded in enlisting him. And he would have done so in the sure and certain hope that the Church would finally discover the right path to take.

In this chapter, however, it is not enough to speculate on what Newman might do in our time in terms of the general characteristics of his mind and spirit. We have to take a more intensive look at his theology and its methodology. As the Newman scholar Ian Ker notes: 'Since the teaching of the Second Vatican Council, which arose out of and which in turn stimulated a return to the sources of the Church's theology, Newman's deeply scriptural and patristic thought has come into its own among Catholic theologians.' And he adds: 'The ecumenical attractions of the most semi-

69

nal of modern Catholic theologians, whose thinking is so markedly un-Scholastic, are also clear enough.'[6]

We looked briefly at Newman's epistemology which represents his search for truth and certitude. We saw that, in his search for truth, the ultimate concern of knowledge, Newman was satisfied that certitude could arise out of a 'convergence of probabilities' even if these were based on a 'collection of weak evidences' which taken together 'makes up a strong evidence'. Another component of his methodology is based on the distinction between an idea (as he understands 'idea') which is purely notional, i.e. purely theoretical, rather than one that is related to the real order of things. This can only be tested by looking for the practical consequences, the correspondence betwen the idea and the reality. This is not a matter of crass pragmatism. It is a conviction that real truth has to reach right down into every facet of human life and activity to transform and conform any idea or theory to the actual situation. What does this or that idea actually do? It is well known that Newman abandoned his theory of the *via media* of Anglicanism because for him it existed 'only on paper' (Preface of 1877).

A more specific example of this and one more to our ecumenical purpose is the way Newman handled the Protestant-Catholic approaches to 'justification by faith'. The old contention between faith and good works has a rather subtle theological foundation. Are there two separate acts of God when God justifies us and makes us holy before God or are these two distinct effects in the one divine act? This was, and to an extent still is a question on which Catholics and some Protestants are divided.[7] Newman was well acquainted with the linguistic biblical basis as to whether the word translated as *righteousness* meant 'counting as righteous' or 'making righteous'. The first meaning could be called *justification* and the second meaning could be called *sanctification* or spiritual renewal. For Newman justification and sanctification are not to be separated, though conceptually undertsood they are distinct, i.e. one is not the other. God always does what God says he is doing. In one moment or act God declares us just and makes us holy. In his search for a *via media* between Protestantism and Roman Catholicism he published his *Lectures on Justification* in 1838.

It is here he argues against both camps, pointing out that one theological camp uses justification in an active sense, the other in a passive sense. Anglicans make no attempt to separate these two senses. Such separation is unreal in terms of the unity in God's action of justifying and sanctifying us. It is not a case of either/or but one of both/and. This provides a new methodology and another alternative theologically speaking. As he said in these lectures of 1838, 'however intelligible each of these answers may be [Protestant and Catholic], neither will be found sufficient and final'.[8] Here Newman was not indulging Anglican comprehensiveness. As Ian Ker notes, Newman does justice to both positions, but transcends them. Both are 'deeply imbedded in a late medieval Scholastic theology of grace which had lost touch with scriptural and patristic sources'. Of Newman's resolution of this faith problem Ker says: 'Its originality lies simply in the rediscovery of the New Testament doctrine of the "indwelling" of the Holy Spirit'.[9] Newman's method here is invaluable for understanding the ecumenical method of dialogue. It takes the problem out of its original polemical setting and transfers it to another one which provides a new perspective or a new hori-

Compare carefully
Newman with the Wesleyan theologian
WB Pope who is somewhat taken with
Wesley & Newman.

zon against which to view it. Ker notes that Newman 'actually changes the nature of the question, which can now be looked at in an altogether different form'. With such an approach he undercut the opposing positions by means of circuminvention. Ker adds that this approach or method 'was to be used later very fruitfully by Newman in tackling very sensitive problems in Roman Catholic ecclesiology. Here it is employed to solve a key point of contention between Protestants and Roman Catholics, and as such suggests its *considerable potential value* as a method in ecumenical theology, to which Newman's book [*Lectures on Justification*] is an early, outstanding contribution'.[10] Newman's own words underline and validate the ecumenical significance of such methodology:

> And thus by tracing farther back the lines of thought on which these apparently discordant views are placed, they are made to converge; they converge, that is, supposing there to be vouchsafed to us an inward divine presence, of which both faith and spiritual renovation are fruits. If such a presence be not vouchsafed, then certainly faith on the one hand, renovation on the other, are the ultimate elements to which our state of righteousness can be respectively referred in the two theologies. But if it be, neither Protestant nor Romanist ought to refuse to admit, and in admitting to agree with each other, that the presence of the Holy Ghost shed abroad in our hearts, the author both of faith and of renewal, this is really that which makes us righteous, and that our righteousness is the possession of that presence.[11]

Here we have a theological rationale and an invitation to dialogue where there is the possibility of finding consensus. In such dialogue ecumenists often find what one refers to as a 'melding of horizons' where divergence can be the occasion of grace and the Churches move to a renewed point of faith where 'the familiar and comfortable boundaries of one's present denominational horizon will need to be expanded into a more universal and thus truly ecumenical horizon'.[12] Newman could well have added that justification by faith becomes real when it is justification by faithfulness to the grace of the Holy Spirit. For both faith by conviction and faith by fidelity to the immediacy of grace in the Holy Spirit assures us of obedience to God's will. Moreover, as Newman would appreciate, it lifts the discussion from the level of the purely notional to a level where it becomes real and relevant for the whole Church.

The issue of authority. Very often ecumenists are asked what is the most fundamental issue to be resolved if divided and separated Christian Churches are to rediscover and achieve full communion and visible unity. My own answer invariably is – authority. John Henry Newman had to face this issue in both the Anglican and Roman Catholic years of his life. He had to reconcile authority with private judgement, setting the parameters of legitimate personal freedom and the exercise of authentic authority. The issue recurs in his Roman Catholic years when he was called to reflect on the delicate questions surrounding infallibility, when he argued his case for a more involved laity in the life of the Church with genuine regard for the *sensus fidelium* of the whole Church. In his Anglican years he had reflected on the internal structures of the Church. He worked to achieve an understanding of the need to create a healthy interaction between the three offices of the Church as prophet, priest, king –

images of Christ's role among us as the one who teaches, who ministers, who commands. He was to experience throughout his life tensions between its teaching role, its pastoral role, and its decision-making role. He believed that such tensions could be good for the life of the Church if there was also sufficient unity among those who played the various roles. All three offices have their proper authority and it is inevitable that from time to time they will challenge one another. The Church is a whole people with emotions and feelings. It is made up of thinkers and those who have a special responsibility for the overall life of the Church. There is need of discernment in the life of the Church and there is need to make this discernment effective for the Church's life and mission. If the principle of authority becomes coterminous with the teachers of the Church, there is the danger of rationalism; if it is coterminous with ministry, it can lead to superstition and false piety, even worship; if it becomes identified only with the hierarchy it may lead to a kind of tyranny. For such unity and balance to be struck all of Newman's peculiar genius and method had to be brought into action. There are two principal areas where his influence reaches down to his own Roman Catholic communion and the other Churches of the ecumenical movement.

Freedom of conscience. One of the pillars of Reformation theology was the authority of conscience and private judgement in the interpretation of Scripture. In his *Letter to the Duke of Norfolk* (1875) Newman carefully nuances his understanding of conscience. Conscience is not a judgement upon any speculative truth, any abstract doctrine, but bears immediately on conduct, on something to be done or not done. It is the refraction of the divine law and divine will. For him

74

conscience is the internal witness of God's existence and the 'aboriginal vicar of Christ'. Conscience is not self-will. It has rights because it has duties. One is always wrong to act contrary to conscience even if one comes to a conscientious conviction by flawed reasoning and the all too human habit of rationalizing. Consequently conscience has to look outward to discover the truth of a situation. Conscience needs to be formed in the context of nature and revelation.

Newman's teaching is summed up in Vatican II's Pastoral Constitution on the Church in the Modern World (§16). Of course the document of that Council which caused a great deal of controversy was the Declaration on Religious Freedom. This Declaration affected the temporal order inasmuch as it removed 'a long standing ambiguity' in relation to the secular and civil order whereby the Church claimed freedom for the Church when Catholics were a minority, but claimed privilege and demonstrated intolerance whenever they constituted a majority. It is important to remember that the Declaration 'opened the way towards new confidence in ecumenical relationships...'[13] Conscience has to respect the discernment process in the Church. It is a mistake all too common to think of this as a discernment confined to one's internal process of self-awareness and conviction. Conscience is a reflection on what is to be done, what is the truth to be discovered in this particular situation, and what is the will of God in this matter. Such a process involves dialogue, a process of careful listening to others with respect for their convictions and an openness to be further convinced and to be changed if the truth demands it. This is what is meant by the formation of conscience or acting out of an informed conscience. There is mutuality in this process. All reconciliation and the formation of individual conscience needs some kind of dialogue or exchange. Dialogue has become a centerpiece in the question of the Churches for Christian unity. This mutuality and respect is reflected in what is now a classical ecumenical statement from the Third World Conference of Faith and Order at Lund in Sweden in 1952: 'Should not our Churches ask themselves whether they are showing sufficient eagerness to enter into conversation with other Churches and whether they should not act together in all matters except those in which deep differences of conviction compel them to act separately.'

Authority. In saying that conscience must look outward if it is to be properly formed and truth perceived, we are faced immediately with the dialectic of freedom and authority, freedom of conscience and authority of the Church. This dialectic remains endemic to the ecumenical movement. Questions of infallibility and primacy, along with forms of episcopal authority remain the chief obstacles to church unity. And they continue to create serious conflicts and tensions within denominations.

Newman's approach is rooted in his high regard for theology and by extension those whose task in the Church is to do theology. This was not an instance of theological elitism bred in the cloisters of Oxford. For Newman, theology is always a servant of faith and religion. By itself it is notional and intellectual. As a servant of faith and religion it has to share their reality and vitality. This reality and vitality lie in revealed religion. If he gave prominence to the work of the theologians, it was because he knew it to be their business to articulate again and again the revelation. Revealed religion is not a matter for private judgement. Theology is a substantive science. Religion cannot stand its ground without theology. Without it doctrine would succumb to the fatuity, the excesses, even the superstitions of devotion when devotion is cut off from its doctrinal and dogmatic moorings.[14] It is in this context, the context of revelation, that the freedom of conscience is truly free (Jn 8:32).

The ecumenical conflict over authority extends to questions of who has the authority and how it is exercised, whether and to what extent it is dispersed or concentrated. Newman's approach to authority was born of a deep conviction that the Church, as God's instrument to convey the revelation of God in Christ to the world, had received the gift of infallibility. In this way only did it make sense to speak of an infallible authority. He affirms this in a letter of 1868:

Thus: I believe the Creed (i.e. as Deposit, I say Creed as more intelligible, since it consists of Articles) was delivered to the Church *with the gift of knowing its true and full meaning*. A divine philosophy is committed to her keeping: not a number of formulas such as a modern pedantic theologian may make theology to consist in, but a system of thought, sui generis in such sense that a mind that was possessed of it, that is, the Church's mind, could definitely and unequivocally say whether this part of it, as traditionally expressed, meant this or that, and whether this or that was agreeable to or inconsistent with it in whole or in part. I wish to hold that there is nothing which the Church has defined or shall define but what an apostle, if asked, would have been fully able to answer and would have answered, as the Church has answered, the one answering by inspiration, the other from its gift of infallibility.[15]

Newman was careful to distinguish between what was of theological opinion and what was a matter of faith. This letter of 1868 (prior to the definition of papal authority in 1870) makes clear that he held papal infallibility 'as a matter of theological opinion' and felt it wrong to set down theological opinions when 'declaring the Church's doctrine as such...'[16] Following the definition of papal infallibility Newman subscribed to it as an article of faith. But following the definition of infallibility he shows his appreciation for the nuances of the definition as when he says: 'Infallibility cannot act outside of a definite circle of thought...'[17] For Newman, papal infallibility finds its context in the infallibility of the Church. Referring to the definition of the Immaculate Conception of 1854 he says that 'Catholics have not come to believe it because it is defined, but it was defined because they believed it.' Regarding non-infallible decisions taken by Church authority, Newman subscribes to the obsequium, the respectful obedience, demanded by such authoritative teaching in this way: 'It must of course be obeyed... and perhaps in process of time it will tacitly recede from its own injunctions...'[18] Such statements are respectful of authority and respectful also of the more complex process of discovering truth. It is the way ecumenists proceed. Ecumenical theology works with the presumption that the discovery of new or the rediscovery of old truths takes time. We live in a world of discovery, development and growth and Christians are not absolved from such processes, even given the revelation of God in Christ. With such an ecumenical methodology it is possible to reconcile freedom and authority, conscience and obedience, what is definite and what is provisional. If Newman failed to establish a real case for the *via media* of Anglicanism, in a real sense he established a methodological *via media* for the ecumencial movement.

Perhaps there is no better place to examine the seeds of this ecumenical methodology than the *Preface* to the third edition of his *Lectures on the Prophetical Office of the Church*. These lectures were first published in 1837 as an Anglican. In this Preface of 1877 as a Roman Catholic we detect more than the apologia of the convert. In the first page of the Preface he says that 'the formal purpose of the volume was, not an attack upon that teaching [Roman Catholic], but the establishment of a doctrine of its own, the Anglican *via media*. It only indirectly comes into collision with the theology of Rome.' He admits the free us of 'hypothesis' in place of 'direct evidence and hard reasoning' which may be true but cannot be proven. Secondly, the method of choosing a *via media*, a middle way, is a 'possible road, lying between a mountain and a morass, to be driven through formidable obstacle... by the boldness and skill of the engineers'. Along with the method of using hypothesis and a middle way Newman acknowledged the legitimate use of logic with its rigorous deductions. None of these methods necessarily lead to the reality and truth about a situation or about another Church. Such methods may well remain at a purely theoretical, notional, intellectual level. Newman insists his purpose to be a search for truth. Speaking in the third person he says:

> Proof was not the main object of his book [*Lectures on the Prophetical Office*]; as far as he aimed at proof in behalf of Anglicanism, he insisted on its reasonableness and consistency: and this, though at the same time he was accusing the theology of Rome of basing itself on consistency to the neglect

79

of truth. He avows that Christianity itself does not in the first place depend on or require argument. He thinks the very preaching of it sufficient to secure its victory. 'Truth', he says, 'has the gift of overcoming the human heart, whether by persuasion or compulsion...' I readily grant in particular that there is much truth in Anglican teaching, and that, so far, it does and will, while it lasts, powerfully affect the multitude of men, to whom it comes; but I cannot allow to the Church of England itself what is true of much of its teaching and many of its teachers, for that teaching and those teachers, who are so effective, know nothing of the via media.

While there is an apologetic tone in all this, this does not rule out its ecumenical value. After all there is some measure of the apologetical in all ecumenical discourse and dialogue of its very nature. Its ecumenical spirit lies in the openness to be corrected by truth as it merges in the process of bringing our thinking and attitudes from the realm of formal logical argument, hypothetical conjecture, and ingenious compromise to a moment of truth which truly transforms a situation, the truth about another person or another Church.

Newman manifests notable ecumenical sensitivity in the way he used the words 'Romanism', 'Romanist', 'Romish' in the Lectures of 1837. His regret is expressed by way of explanation that 'the more he had these feelings towards it [admiration, reverence, love and gratitude], the more he needed a word which would distinguish what he accepted from what scandalized him'. By this Newman referred to what he called a 'recurring contrast... between the theological side of Roman teaching and its political and popular

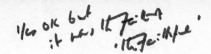

side'. It was this political and popular side of Roman Catholicism he had in mind when he used such terminology as 'Romanist' and 'Romanism' and 'Romish'.

Internal authority. Ecumenism has to deal, however respectfully, with the internal problems and tensions of denominations. Such problems and tensions have their effect on the renewal of Churches for unity and mission. These remain essential components of the ecumenical movement, i.e. renewal for mission and unity. Unity for mission would remain unreal and notional if particular Churches failed to set up a programme of internal renewal. Not least of such internal problems is the understanding of what it means to be the Church here and now in our present situation. We have to remember that for Newman theology is 'the fundamental and regulating principle of the whole Church system...' and 'is commensurate with revelation'. Hence ecumenism is very much exercised by various theologies of the Church and how authority is structured and actually works in these various conceptions of the Church. Another way of expressing the central ecumenical question is: How do you understand the teaching office of the Church? So when we come to develop relationships with other Churches any one Church has to be very much aware of how authority works in these Churches. Newman is helpful here, particularly in developing relations between Anglican and Roman Catholics. For he is concerned with the inter-relationships of the teaching, pastoral, and governing functions of Church life as these reflect the office of prophet, priest and king, the traditional way of understanding the mission of Our Lord. Within episcopally structured Churches there is the tension of theologian and bishop. The former shares and assists in the teaching office while the latter holds a key role in how the Church is governed and its teaching stated. Both are means to undergird an effective pastoral function of the Chruch as a mature body of Christians with a sense of being called into a community of faith in order to witness to Christ and bring his message to the world.

Because Newman was steeped in this sense of Church he brought his unusual energies of heart and mind to the task of striking a balance between the threefold functions of these ecclesial structures as prophet (teacher), priest (pastor), king (legislator and teacher of faith). Later, ecumenists would have to be engaged on all three fronts – one with other Churches, one with internal problems of renewal, one concerned with the Church's mission in the world. Much of Newman's life was spent on the second front.

As a Roman Catholic Newman was sensitive to the difficulties experienced in other Churches with claims and practices of his own Church. He was aware that such were willing to ascribe a measure of holiness to the Roman Catholic Church. There were those who were willing to acknowledge much theological soundness in this Church. But these very same people accused the Roman Catholic Church of ambition, craft, and the cruelty of political power. In the Preface of 1877 he admitted this as giving 'so much offence to Protestants'. With this in mind he set out to explain the interaction of the threefold office in Roman Catholic ecclesiology. He says: 'Arduous as are the duties involved in these three offices to discharge one by one, much more arduous are they to adminster, when taken in combination.' Further he notes that 'each of the three [teaching, ministry, governance] has its separate scope and direction; each has its own interests to promote and further; each has to find room for the claims of the other two; and each will find its own line of action influenced and modified by the others, nay, sometimes in a particular case the necessity of the others converted into a rule of duty for itself.' Here we have a statement entirely relevant to our ecumenical situation today as the Churches look for internal renewal and ecumenical partnership.

Much of the remainder of the Preface of 1877 is taken up with a description and apologia for the interaction of these three offices in the course of the Church's history. Because of the substantive role played by theology in the Church's history and in the development of its doctrine Newman 'shows how little authority has interfered with the freedom of theologians'. But Ian Ker continues by saying that 'beneath the apparent movement of the argument, there runs a contrary, stronger undercurrent, for what really concerns Newman... is that what was true of the past is no longer true of the present. But... he is also stating with great deliberateness his considered view on the crucial balance to be maintained between theology and the teaching authority of the Church'.[19]

The tension between theology and an infallible teaching office has not disappeared. Indeed it has reasserted itself in our time. While this tension cannot be identified entirely as a Roman Catholic tension, it remains a principal obstacle in the search for Christian unity inclusive of Roman Catholicism. All Churches experience at some time or other the tension between authority and theological teaching and preaching. If we are to take the prophetical office of the Church seriously, we have to take theology and theologians seriously. For Newman this is so because theology 'is commensurate with revelation and revelation is the initial and essential idea of Christianity... the subject matter, the formal cause, the expression of the prophetical office...' He is referring here to the function of theology, not the responsibility of theologians to do their theology in essential unity with the episcopal and pastoral offices. He goes on pressing the point by saying that the prophetical [teaching office] has *created* the two other offices of ministry and governance 'and it has in a certain sense a power of jurisdiction over these offices... theologians being ever in request and in employment in keeping within bounds both the political and popular elements in the Church's constitution – elements which... are far more liable to excess and corruption, and are ever struggling to liberate themselves from those restraints which are in truth necessary for their well-being'. Yet he is careful to add that 'theology cannot always have its own way' for it is 'too hard, too intellectual, too exact, to be always equitable, or to be always compassionate; and it sometimes has a conflict or overthrow, or has to consent to a truce or compromise, in consequence of the rival force of religious sentiment or ecclesiastical interests; and sometimes in great matters, sometimes in unimportant'.[20] Tensions between official teaching of a non-infallible nature and the freedom of theologians to explore the realm of faith would not come as a surprise to Newman. The offices of the Church are not mutually exclusive whether we speak of functions or the persons authorized to exercise them from the very nature of the Church. Those who exercise *episcope* or governance are also teachers of the faith. Both theologians and those exercising *episcope* must be open to the experience and needs of those who exercise pastoral ministry in very local and particular situations. Functions and persons frequently overlap and all are connected in the one body of Christ. In the spirit of

Newman there will always be the need to match theological pace with the praxis and official positions taken by the Church, or as Newman put it in the Preface of 1877 'to make her [the Church] sacerdotal office keep step with her prophetical'.

Untidy ecumenism. The ecumenical movement does not fit neatly into our denominational structures. The movement is thus uneven, untidy, indeed anomalous. It seems little more than the proverbial 'optional extra'. The point of departure and the one factor which gives cohesion and realism to ecumenism is the reality of the one baptism into the one Christ. In the Preface to the third edition of the *Lectures on the Prophetical Office of the Church* Newman reflected on the anomalies and irregularities, indeed the conflicts of the Church in the early centuries over issues such as baptism versus re-baptism, the ordination of heretics, schismatics, the validity of simoniacal ordinations. These conflicts and issues involved popes and eminent Fathers and Doctors of the Church. He reflects particularly on baptism and specifically on the question of recognizing heretical baptism. Newman describes such baptized heretics as 'children of the Church'. Moreover, he says they were 'preachers of the truth of Christ to the heathen, since there is no religious sect without truth in it, and it would be truth which the heathen did not know'. Such a position does not exactly make Newman an ecumenist as we understand the term today. In an ecumenical age we tend to cringe at the rather free use of terms like 'heretic' and 'heathen' and indeed feel very uncomfortable with what came naturally in a nineteenth century context. Nonetheless, Newman's approach and words indicate an openness to and recognition of truth wherever it appears. Such openness informs all genuine ecumenism.

Newman did not have the advantage of a clear principle which would enable him to state unequivocally
that the union between Churches was a real though
imperfect communion. For Roman Catholics at least
this was a direct gift of the Spirit through the Second
Vatican Council, a council often called 'Newman's
council' But perhaps we can recognize an affinity for
such an ecclesiological principle when he attributes
the 'exuberant birth of strange rites and doctrines,
which suddenly burst into life all round Christianity
on its start' as 'one of the striking evidences of the
wondrous force of the Christian idea, and of its pen-
etrating influence...' He points out also that Pope
Stephen upheld the validity of heretical baptisms – not
on the basis of expediency but upon Tradition. Further
and remarkably he says: 'To cut off such cautious
baptism from the Church was to circumscribe her
range of subjects and to impair her catholicity.' Eighty-
seven years later Vatican II concentrated on this last
point precisely when the principle of catholicity became a working principle for Roman Catholic participation in the ecumenical movement:

> Nevertheless, the divisions among Christians pre-
> vent the Church from effecting the fullness of
> catholicity proper to her in those of her children
> who, though joined to her by baptism, are yet sepa-
> rated from full communion with her. Furthermore,
> the Church herself finds it more difficult to express
> in her actual life her full catholicity in all its aspects
> (Decree on Ecumenism, 4).

Ecumenism has created a remarkable spirit of tolerance and good will among Christians. Christians feel
more and more comfortable together in worship and

social projects. Yet so many ask how the Churches move ahead to a deeper Christian unity whereby the Church can be seen to be a communion of Churches living in full communion, diverse in traditions and practices, but credibly and organically united. The way forward seems to lie in a renewed sense of the importance to manifest the catholicity of the Church as a Church whose orientation is towards the whole and the wholeness of human life on this planet. Newman's ecclesiology has gone a long way in pointing the way.

For the vast majority in our Churches ecumenism in this catholic sense has yet to be realized. And the movement itself has yet to be received into the bloodstream of Church life. Formal commitments have been made but are yet to be made real in the actual praxis of the Churches – beyond paper and beyond the dialogues of experts. The identity of the Christian Church becomes unmistakeable when we cease to identify only with our denominational structures. When this is said ecumenists leave themselves open to the older accusation of breeding indifference to Church membership, of encouraging a kind of churchless Christianity. In fact ecumenism is quite opposed to this. It is a rediscovery of real Church unity by stages and by a convergence in life and worship to a point whereby unity and diversity enhance the catholic character of the Church for its mission in Christ's name to the world. The Church cannot change in essence, but must change whatever no longer serves this mission in the world. It is common knowledge that Christian disunity obscures this mission and witness. It is sometimes referred to as a scandal – as indeed it is for many young Christians and for others to whom we expound the Gospel.

I wonder if it is

John Henry Newman in his Anglican years challenged the Church of England to rediscover its catholicity, indeed he declared its mission to represent 'a theology, Catholic but not Roman' and added that this was a special reason 'why her members should be on the watch for opportunities of bringing out and carrying into effect her distinctive character'.[21] He regarded this as the special mission of the English Church to both Protestants and Roman Catholics. Later he would discover the catholicity of Roman Catholicism in all its cultural and historical diversity through the ages. All the Churches of both East and West lay claim to catholicity – either in its fullness, or in part. All need to deepen and make real and visible their claim to a truly catholic character. All confess in one way or another membership in one, holy, catholic and apostolic Church. Indeed the principal aim of the ecumenical movement is to rediscover and witness to the catholicity of the Church – a home, an *oikos* for all people. Newman anticipated such a movement when he wrote in the Preface of 1877:

> If the Church is to be regal, a witness for heaven, unchangeable amid secular changes, if in every age she is to hold her own, and proclaim as well as profess the truth, if she is to thrive without or against the civil power, if she is to be resourceful and self-recuperative under all fortunes, she must be more than holy and apostolic; she must be catholic... and all with a view to the life, health, and strength of Christianity, and the salvation of souls.

It is then a sense of regaining, renewing, even manifesting a richer catholicity than heretofore experienced in the Church's history which will provide the Churches with the motivation they need to explore the theological and spiritual dynamic of the ecumenical movement. The immediate need in all our Churches is an awakening of the threefold office of teaching, preaching and leadership to motivate the members of the various Churches to a new consciousness of the Church's catholicity. If this threefold ministry is renewed as such, the motivation and the understanding of what ecumenism means for the Church will be assured. It was a challenge in Newman's time and it is a challenge in our time, an even greater one. Catholicity is not a static mark of the Church. It is dynamic for the Church to be faithful to her mandate to bring the Gospel, the good news of Christ, to the world until its consummation. The stability of the Church comes from the assurance of Christ to be with us. Its dynamism comes from the promise of the Spirit to lead us into all truth. As such the ecumenical movement is directly related to the catholicity of the Christian Church for, as Newman said, 'in this ever-dying, ever-nascent world... to be stationary is to lose ground, and to repose is to fail'.[22]

NOTES

1. *Newman after a Hundred Years*, ed. Ian Ker and Alan G. Hill, Oxford: Clarendon Press, 1990.
2. The conclusion of Newman's Preface to the 1877 edition of *Lectures on the Prophetical Office of the Church*, first published in 1837. This 1877 Preface is important as his Roman Catholic reflection on what was written in his Anglican years. Hence it contains value for our ecumenical interpretation of Newman. Hereafter it will be referred to as the Preface of 1877.
3. H. Francis Davis, 'Newman and the Theology of the Living Word' in *Newman: Studien Sechste Folge*, Herausgegeben Von Heinrich Fries und Werner Becker, Nurnberg: Glock and Lutz, 1964, p. 173.
4. Ibid. p. 174.

5. Ibid. p. 174-6.
6. Ian Ker, *The Achievement of John Henry Newman*, first published by the Univeristy of Notre Dame Press, USA, 1990. Available also from the Collins Publishing Group, London 1990, p. 96.
7. The Anglican-Roman Catholic International Commission (ARCIC II) in its agreed statement entitled *Salvation and the Church* has responded to this question in paragraphs 12-18.
8. *Lectures on Justification*, second ed., Rivington & Parker, 1840, Lecture 6, p. 151.
9. Ker, op. cit., pp. 108-9. Cf Lecture 6 on Justification, esp. the final paragraph.
10. Ibid. pp. 108-9.
11. *Lectures on Justification*, 6, edition cited, p. 152.
12. John Ford, 'Bilateral Conversations and Denominational Horizons', *Journal of Ecumenical Studies*, vol. 23, no. 3 (1986), pp. 518-528.
13. Cf John Courtney Murray's introduction to the Declaration *Dignitatis Humanae* in the Abbot ed. of the Council Documents.
14. Cf *A Grammar of Assent*, ch. 5.
15. Cf *Journal of Theological Studies*, Vol. 9 (1958), pp. 329-335.
16. Ibid. p. 329.
17. Cf the *Apologia*, ch. 5 where he deals with the question of infallibility in the context of the Church's infallibility.
18. Ibid.
19. Cf Ian Ker, op. cit., pp. 128-131. Ker is drawing from the *Apologia*, not the Preface of 1877.
20. Preface of 1877.
21. Cf Newman's introductory lecture on *Lectures on the Prophetical Office of the Church*.
22. Preface of 1877.

Chapter 5

Receiving the ecumenical movement

There is no need here to review the history of the ecumenical movement. It is well documented from 1910 onwards. It is necessary to reassess the movement which is a movement towards Church unity for the sake of the Church's mission by means of renewal in Church life. However, one point of recent history must be mentioned. This is the official entry into the movement by the Roman Catholic Church. On 21 November 1964 the Decree on Ecumenism of Vatican II officially committed that Church to ecumenism. Reflecting on the Decree twenty-five years later, James Crumley, the former presiding bishop of the former Lutheran Church in America (now integrated within the Evangelical Lutheran Church in America) expressed his belief that the Decree was 'even more important than the formation of some of the ecumenical organizations that had been hard at work for several years'.[1] In the same issue of *Ecumenical Trends*, Günther Gassmann, director of the Faith and Order Commission of the World Council of Churches, remarked that the Decree 'has opened up new ecclesiological developments which have taken on their own dynamic and ecumenical logic'.[2] Again in the same issue of *Ecumenical Trends* Susan Wood, an associate professor of theology at St Mary College, Leavenworth, Kansas, says that in the twenty-five years since Vatican II there has been 'a growing consensus that an ecclesiology of communion is the central and fundamental idea of the Council's documents. With special reference to its use in the Decree on Ecumenism she notes that the communion/*koinonia* concept is central and fundamental because 'it defines the Church in terms of those elements of faith and grace that create community rather than ecclesiastical structures; secondly, it allows for degrees of unity among the various Churches' and is therefore 'a much more elastic concept than Church membership'.[3] The Decree on Ecumenism represents a new stage of growth for the ecumenical movement. Edinburgh 1910 and Rome 1964 are markers in the growth of the movement.

Since 1910 the Churches have been challenged by ecumenism. In the early years unity for the sake of mission was the main feature of the movement and rightly remains so. Yet for many Churches this remained a co-operative venture blessed by new and sincere tolerance united to mutual respect. At the theological level a lot of comparative ecclesiology was done in which Churches sought to identify themselves to other Churches. Now these stages of growth are essential. At the level of social and missionary activity co-operation was and remains indispensable. At the theological level dialogue and self-identification remain vital to the movement. Dialogue has as its primary goal to get and give a fair perception of one another's Churches in their history and practice. But to remain at these stages of ecumenical growth would be to stunt the growth of the movement. Other issues have to be raised, especially those which continue to divide the Churches. Moreover, hard questions have to be asked: How much agreement and disagreement exists among us? How basic are these agreements and disagreements doctrinally speaking? And then, if the Christian Churches acknowledge their obligation to seek the unity Christ prayed for to ensure his mission in the world (Jn 17:21), what is the nature of the unity we ought to be looking for? What kind of unity? What model of Church unity can we agree is the right one? These questions with their provisional answers ensure growth and development in ecumenism. The trouble is they often remain at a stratospheric level. They never become the questions the whole Church ought to be asking and concerned about. The fact that they are theological questions indicates a significant shift in ecumenism. Yet the big question remains: How is ecumenism going to enter the life of the Churches in terms of the ordinary life of these Churches? How is it to be received as a dimension of church life in all Churches by the general membership of those Churches? Theological progress is such that the theologians are far ahead of church leaders and rank and file Church membership. Some might feel they are too far ahead. The Faith and Order Conference at Montreal in 1963 adopted a new method which accounts for such progress in ecclesial bridge-building. Rather than engaging in comparative views of the Church as they presently are, the Conference felt that the theologians ought to look more carefully at what sort of unity the Church had prior to the major schisms between East and West, between Protestantism and Catholicism when there was essential visible unity and communion between the Churches. At Montreal it was felt that such a method would enable theologians to work more closely together in order to construct a vision of what the Church ought to be.

Another factor in the growth of ecumenism was an ever growing sense of the need for denominations to renew themselves from within. A new sense of urgency was felt, especially in the wake of Vatican II, to create more community life and less institutional life in the Churches after the model of Acts 4:32,35. The Church as a communion and the unity of the Churches as a communion of communions became a working model. Ecumenists felt there was no point in looking for church union, or, as it was sometimes referred to, ecclesiastical joinery, without this renewed sense of communion and community. *Koinonia*, the Greek word used to convey this new feeling, entered theological dialogue and ordinary idiom in a new way. No one wanted a Church of either Frankensteinian or Constantinian proportions. No one wanted a bionic Church. Ecumenists and others were looking for a caring, sharing community of faith with some institutional streamlining and updating. *Aggiornamento* was often used to express the renewal going on in the Churches. That word was rich because it meant that the Churches were looking to a new day, a new time, a new unity for the Churches. *Ressourcement* was also used at this time to indicate that renewal meant getting back to the roots and resources of the Church's life as a community of faith. So renewal meant going back to an earlier understanding of the Church and going down to the spiritual sources or springs of its real life and meaning in the world. It became more and more evident that the Churches were opting for spiritual and structural renewal before the unity of the Church for its mission could be fully realized. Thus *renewal* became the new factor in the ecumenical equation.

However, the equation remains unsolved. Another factor has to be introduced. This situation brings us up to our own time in the ecumenical movement. The introduction of this factor will most probably engage ecumenists for a much longer period of time. To set times and dates would be a great presumption. This factor is *reception*. How is ecumenism to be received by the Churches and Church membership *as a whole*. There is of course official commitment to ecumenism by most mainline Churches. I am speaking of the commitment to seek visible, credible unity. Yet it is very doubtful that there is a real will to put ecumenism at the top of the list of priorities or even move it up the list. More often it is at the bottom of the list, almost as an optional extra, if time is left over, or some token acknowledgement seems in order. Most members of the Churches do not have an ecumenical vision or open hearts to seek 'the unity Christ wills by the means he chooses', as Paul Couturier expressed it. It is supposed, at very least, to be a dimension of church life, but more often it seems to be indefinitely postponed, a dimension of another life in another world, or confined to theological discourse. So the issue and factor of *reception* arises. With *unity mission* and *renewal* reception of the ecumenical vision of one Church for one world by the whole Church is the new challenge to the growth and fulfillment of the ecumenical movement.

Reception. Reception has been called the new 'holy word' of the ecumenical movement. It has a long history in theology and church history. It even had a secular origin in the field of jurisprudence. In this sense it referred to how the newly formed peoples of Europe took the Roman legal system into their own structures of government. For our purpose there are two ways of understanding *reception* in the life of the Church. There is the older classical understanding. This is the acceptance of a doctrinal statement or Church decision formulated by a council of the Church at local, regional or world level. Then there is its present ecumenical usage. This involves the acceptance of the responsibility at all levels of Church life to work for the restoration of Christian unity and likewise to accept the measure of consensus already achieved in the ecumenical movement through dialogue and various statements of agreement or convergence produced therein. The two meanings of reception are not unrelated for both are used in relation to the need to maintain the level of unity already possessed by the Church, all the while working towards a more perfect and complete unity of the Church. This will always be an ongoing task for the Church, even in the event of visible church unity as it was before the major schisms in the East and the West. The unity of the Church is always susceptible of deeper and more visible unity. Both meanings of the word *reception* are rooted in Scripture where we sense the struggle of the Christian Churches of the early centuries to manifest their real visible unity in Christ.[4]

Because of the extraordinary theological progress in the ecumenical movement a new danger has arisen. If the members of our Churches by and large are not *receiving* the ecumenical movemnet as a movement of the Holy Spirit, the consequences for the Church's mission, its life and witness can only be described as a diminishment for the cause of Christ. Ecumenism becomes a luxury for theologians, a talking shop for church leaders and ecumenical middle managers, the enthusiasm of a small group, an option for the elite, the educated. It remains a movement in name only, marginalized and optional, a spiritual luxury quite dispensable. In saying this it does not mean there is no room for very careful discernment in the reception process. As I have said, there is no need to fix times and dates or issue ultimatums. As J.M. Tillard says: 'Everything depends on the manner in which the fruits of the current theological discussions are "received" by the communities involved.'[5] Tillard advocates such care in the matter of reception when he speaks of agreed statements or convergence documents such as those coming from the Anglican-Roman Catholic International Commission or the Lima Document of 1982. Since the communion of Churches is the goal of any ecumenical endeavour, even theologians have to beware of seeming to agree without sufficiently testing what they feel is their common faith and agreement on certain doctrinal matters, e.g. baptism, eucharist, ministry. As Tillard says: 'The essential requirement is a collective conversion to the claims of the apostolic faith *as such.*' Such agreements 'must be given to the reality and certainty of faith rather than to the goodwill and the desire to re-establish cordial relations'.[6]

So reception is a matter of testing the apostolic faith behind each ecumenical agreement. When such documents come before the general membership of the Churches it is a moment for referring such agreements to the *sense of faith in the faithful* or what Newman called for – consulting the faithful in matters of doctrine. Such documents of agreement and convergence move out of the hands of theologians into those of church leaders and synods of a representative nature. While they bear the theological authority of those who produced them, they do not automatically become official Church positions to be received. They must also be passed on to clergy and laity in local congregations, not only for information, but for study and discernment as well. In this way *Churches as Churches* enter the reception process. The ecumenical movement is asking for just this – the reception of the fruit of dialogue and discernment to enrich further dialogue and discernment in order to make ecumenism a spirit and reality for church life. Every participating group must 'assess the faith and practices of its associates' as well as its own faith. As Tillard says, 'each Church has to challenge the other.' Reception is related to the development of doctrine inasmuch as it is a re-reading, a re-evaluation and a re-confessing of the apostolic faith itself. This process of reception makes it clear that the unity we are seeking in the end is not 'a fusion of all parties in one and the same pattern of ecclesial living; rather they are aiming for a communion of all in one and the same faith, with room for diversity of form and practice...'[7]

This concern for the apostolic faith as a norm is always joined to a rigorous examination and exploration of how other Churches respond in terms of their understanding of what fidelity to the apostolic faith means for them. This process of reception has been admirably exemplified by the Lima Document on Baptism, Eucharist and Ministry (known as BEM). Those who wrote the document, a hundred and twenty theologians from mainline Churches, expected some *response* from the Churches. They were not asking for an immediate reception of the text. *Response is an early stage of the reception process.* Hence the Faith and Order Commission of the World Council of Churches asked a series of questions of the Churches. The Commission wanted to know:

9. mainly like it.

1. the extent to which your Church can recognize in this text the faith of the Church through the ages;

2. the consequences your Church can draw from the text for its relations and dialogues with other Churches, particularly with those Churches which also recognize the text as an expression of apostolic faith;

3. the guidance your Church can take from this text for its worship, educational, ethical and spiritual life and witness;

4. the suggestions your Church can make for the ongoing work of Faith and Order as it relates the material of Baptism, Eucharist and Ministry to its long-range research project 'Towards the common expression of the apostolic faith today'.

From this we can see that the reception process is vital in the search for unity, if the search is an honest one and not another academic exercise or talking-shop. The Church is by nature a receptive Church. Its grace and truth are received from the Lord Jesus (Jn 1:17-18). Paul asks pointedly of the Corinthian community: What have you that you did not receive? (1 Cor 4:7; Rom 11:35-36; 15:7). As each has received a gift, employ it for one another, as good stewards of God's varied grace (1 Pet 4:10). In working to restore visible, credible Christian unity we are asked to develop this spirit of receptivity as Churches and as individual Christians. The present ecumenical perception is that this is the moment to stress reception as the missing factor in the ecumenical equation. The work of theological dialogue has left denominations relatively untouched and unmoved. Some would say that the theologians have gone too far ahead of judicatory bodies and the faithful members of the Churches in general. Ecumenism ought to slow down. On the other hand, the theologians and brokers of the movement feel stymied. They are often the objects of suspicion as though they were selling out the true faith or compromising conscientiously held convictions. It fact the principles from which they work and theologize are such that they are intended to renew faith while respecting conscientiously held convictions. To remedy this situation *reception* of the ecumenical movement as part of Church life three things are needed: an ecumenical spirituality, formation as Christians, a renewed sense of the faith in the faithful. All these together are meant to function in the body of Christ. We need to look at each of these in some detail.

Spirituality. This demands more than saying some prayers for unity, especially during the Week of Prayer for Christian Unity (18-25 January). Prayer for Christian unity must be accompanied by conversion and a sincere practice of Christian faith. Conversion entails a sense of urgency in this matter of Christian unity. It involves getting a fair perception of where other Christians are in their Churches. It means turning away from drawing caricatures or misrepresenting other Churches in their beliefs and practices. In this matter of conversion J.M. Tillard speaks of a 'collective conversion to the claims of the apostolic faith *as such*'.[8] Christians are in dialogue and together in all kinds of joint activities because of a shared vision – their essential oneness in Christ. Such a vision demands holiness and justice among Christians and towards others. This is the ecumenical movement. It is more than a matter of Church policy or a matter of politeness. Ecumenism is an essential part of Christian spirituality. Reception is under the direction of the Holy Spirit. The Holy Spirit enables separated Churches to welcome new and fresh expressions, even rediscoveries of a common faith. It is the work of the Spirit which enables Christians to recognize the results of ecumenical dialogue and co-operation to be in some continuity with apostolic faith. It is likewise the Spirit's business to help the Churches harmonize the renewed insights arising from ecumenical relationships with the inherited life and polity of their own denominations. This of course is rooted in a sound doctrine of the centrality of the Holy Spirit in the life of the Church. Reception is really a re-reception of the Christian Tradition. This is the continuing task of the Church under the Holy Spirit. When the Roman Catholic Church acknowledged the ecumenical movement and received it officially, it described the movement in the Decree on Ecumenism as 'under the influence of the grace of the Holy Spirit' (nos. 1 and 4). The former Lutheran Church in America, responding to the BEM document, said that 'reception ultimately will not be a matter of documents, but a renewed people under the Spirit expressing their unity in Christ'. And in the last stage of their own ecclesial life, prior to becoming part of the Evangelical Lutheran Church in America, these Lutherans of LCA voted to 'continue the ongoing process of the reception of BEM within the Church'.[9]

Reception, then, is first and foremost a spiritual process. This does not absolve Churches from reaching decisions or responding to the results of formal theological dialogue. Yet, reception demands more than response. As Churches we are asked to receive from one another the gifts granted our denominations by the Spirit in those long periods of mutual exclusion and separation. Ecumenism signals a new inclusiveness whereby we mutually give and receive what the Holy Spirit has been effecting in the Churches through the centuries. Lukas Vischer says: 'For such a reception to take place Churches are called to develop a "spirituality of reception", a readiness for reforms and structures of common decision making. Every consensus invites the Churches to express jointly the *single* tradition in their midst and newly make it their own.'[10]

Christian formation. Intimately related to the reception process in its spirituality is the need for ecumenical formation. Here I am not thinking principally about education in the principles or material content of ecumenism. I am thinking about a quality of spirit, a benevolence beyond mere toleration, a way of reacting to what is happening in our Churches as a result of their official commitment to ecumenism. Formation is not synonymous with *information*. Formation conveys a sense that the Churches realize something significant has happened because of such a commitment. It has to enter the life of these Churches as the 'great new fact of our era' to use the expression of William Temple in his enthronement sermon as Archbishop of Canterbury in 1942. Formation means we are prepared to move beyond where we are at present in our Churches. Formation in ecumenism gives a clear understanding that we are in a convergence process leading to visible organic unity, full communion with legitimate diversity, which diversity is such that it manifests the catholic nature of the Church.

For such formation to be positive and practical there is needed a spiritual interpretation of ecumenical events. There are two stages in the formation of this 'spiritual hermeneutic' as it is sometimes called. The first is the *development of principles* which enable a denomination to become actively engaged in the ecumenical movement. For example, when the Roman Catholic Church received the ecumenical movement officially at the time of Vatican II it recognized some measure of ecclesiality in other Churches. It had to reformulate its theological thinking in this respect. This led to new relationships with the Anglican Communion, the Orthodox Church, and the Churches of the Reformation. It was able to do so in virtue of a principle that there are various degrees of imperfect communion among the Christian Churches and ecclesial communities. Other principles were used as well and are found in the first chapter of the Decree on Ecumenism. Without such principles the practice of ecumenism would be virtually impossible.

The second stage in the formation of this spiritual hermeneutic is a *spiritual reading of ecumenical texts*. By this is meant reading such documents as the ARCIC I Final Report, the Lima (BEM) Document, the Lutheran-Roman Catholic Statement on Justification in the same spirit of openness in which they were written. It means reading such documents with some understanding of what methodology operated in the group producing the report, or document, or statement. We do not prejudge such ecumenical results by principles developed and pre-established within our own particular denominational frame of reference. The only norm to be used is the one we have been asked to use in reading the BEM document, viz. to what extent is your Church able to recognize in this text the faith of the Church throughout the ages? Consequently, information is not enough. Information of course is indispensable in the reception process. But it must lead to a genuine spiritual response which *forms* our theological thinking with a spiritual understanding of ecumenism. Such a spiritual response transforms our attitudes and outlook towards other Churches. It affects the very way we read and respond to ecumenical texts and information. This spiritual awareness leads to a renewed sense of faith, that special feeling or instinct for faith we experience in ourselves and in others as true believers formed by Scripture and Tradition through the ages, what we have learned to call the *sensus fidei in fidelibus*, a sense of faith in the faithful.

Sensus fidelium. One of the unanswered questions put by today's ecumenists is: How does theological agreement, consensus, or convergence become the property of the Churches? How does general Church membership take ownership of developing ecumenical relationships? To begin to answer such questions one has to stress the relationship between the reception process and the *sensus fidelium*. The latter is the action of the Holy Spirit in the hearts of believers. This sense of faith in the faithful 'is aroused and sustained by the spirit of truth' (*Lumen Gentium*, 12). Addressing the then Lutheran Church in America at the Toronto Convention of 1984 Cardinal Willebrands spoke at length about the relationship of reception with the *sensus fidelium*. He said:

> If we speak about the faith in an ecumenical dialogue and arrive at a joint understanding of the faith, does this not mean that the Spirit of God is at work within us and is going to ensure reception? It is for the Church as a whole: The counsellor, the Holy Spirit, whom the Father will send in my name, will teach you all things (Jn 14:26).[11]

Unless we are to retreat to a very narrow denominationalism we have to take this grace of the Holy Spirit into our Churches. This grace, as all grace, is not 'cheap'. In responding to such documents as the Final Report of ARCIC I or BEM there has to be a critical evaluation in the light of the apostolic faith. Moreover, in receiving the results of such high-level dialogue the process of reception requires participating Churches to examine their own fidelity to the apostolic tradition. Each Church is free to challenge other Churches as to their fidelity to this tradition. Each Church is free to challenge other Churches in their fidelity to the faith as practised in the day to day life of those Churches.

Getting to the *sensus fidelium* takes time and makes demands on all the Churches. But as part of the reception process there is revealed a new and larger context for the truths that lie behind both ecumenical and denominational formulations of faith.[12] In the end our faith will be more firmly grounded, more mature, a better reflection of its true quality as a gift of God.

The desire for unity, *votum unitatis*, means that we want the Church to be all it is called to be according to the mind of Christ and the will of God. This *votum* or desire is expressed by our ever growing numbers of Christians who live, work and pray together as members of one body, the body of Christ. This *votum unitatis* recognizes and receives what the Spirit has been doing in the Churches during the years of separation and schism. It recognizes new situations and developments aside older gifts. Such diversity and mixture of old and new gifts in the life of the Church can only be a plus for the catholicity of the Church in this reintegrated Church unity. When we desire Christian unity it ought to be a desire for a more perfect unity which allows a variety of expressions of the one faith in doctrine and theology, in liturgy and culture. As Robert Butterworth said: 'Pluriformity is not an unfortunate concession to human weakness, nor is the Christian revelation receivable and expressible in one way only.'[13]

Closely related to this desire for unity is a sense of being faithful *with* other faithful members of other Churches. J.M. Tillard expresses this point well:

As long as they remain divided, unable to live together a true community of faith expressed in the sharing of a common Eucharist, they are not what they are supposed to be. They are all marked by this failure, even if some are convinced they possess everything that is required to be truly the Church of God. For this mission does not consist in an *addition* of faithfulness but in a *common* faithfulness.[14]

Essential to the reception process is the practical involvement of the lay membership of our Churches. Involvement means more than a few desultory study groups for a few mildly interested or loyal parishioners. Pastoral leadership has to be such that the local congregation *as a whole* has some experience of the unity of the Church 'even now, but not yet'. Only when such experience can be had by a notable number of the faithful – lay and clerical – in all Churches can the reception process flourish. There has to be an honest-to-God *sensus fidelium*, a real growth in faith on the part of the faithful. An Orthodox theologian, John Zizioulas, sums it up accurately: 'The last word is with the Churches and not with individuals... But Churches mean communities structured in a particular way. In an event of communion, it does not mean either dispersed individuals or isolated authorities.'[15] Since reception is a matter of spirituality, inasmuch as it is the recognition of the action of the Holy Spirit in the whole Chruch, everything which feeds into the process – authority, discipline, liturgy, preaching and teaching, the life of devotion and practices of piety – all must be united to a sincere will for Christian unity.

We have been considering the tri-dimensional nature of the reception process. The success of the process will be ensured if this spiritual, formative, total membership commitment is held together. Ecumenism remains a movement in which church leaders, theologians, pastors and teachers will need consummate skill and sensitivity in handling the ecumenical dimension of church life. Reception is a new stage in the overall movement towards Christian unity for the sake of the Church's mission. And reception cannot take place apart from a collective interior renewal of church life. This process relies on a collective perception that the ecumenical movement is a movement of the Holy Spirit. Officially and theologically the Churches are asked to *receive* what it is the Spirit is saying to the Churches. This perception is rooted in the daily experience of faithful Christians in parishes and congregations, in the so-called 'grassroots movements' taking place in our Churches. It is an interaction between podium, pew and pulpit which allows the Church to be both *listening* and *teaching* Church. Reception is a shared experience of the whole people of God celebrating and living out their unity in Christ. This interaction is simply a recognition that faith is received from God to be handed on for the life of the world from age to age. As we do this it is developed and new insights garnered which enhance and enrich faith. And as we do this we grow as a people with a distinct life and mission in human history. What we discover in one age is connected with what has been discovered in other ages and all discoveries become the heritage of a future age. The task of communicating this apostolic faith, i.e. the faith received from Christ in the mystery of the Church, is a task for all Christians. This is reflected in a description we have of how the decisions of the first ecumenical council of Jerusalem were reached by 'the apostles and elders, *with the whole Church*' (Acts 15:22). Whatever models and methods we speculate on as more or less suitable to express our Christian unity as we envisage it in the future, this apostolic faith remains the lodestar for us. Our efforts to reconstitute a visible, credible church unity represents our fidelity to the injunction 'to contend for the faith which was once for all delivered to the saints' (Letter of Jude, v. 3).

Whenever the Church moves into a new, unprecedented age or situation it has to take on a mood of discovery and a spirit of discernment. But, it has also to take on a spirit of receptivity, an attitude of being radically open to the newness of life we are asked to walk in (Rom 6:4) under the promise of God to make all things new (Rev 21:4). Avery Dulles says that reception 'belongs, or should belong, to the very kernel of any sound Christian theology' for 'theology is a methodical reflection on faith and faith is something that must be received'. In the same place he goes on to say that establishing a theological rationale for the reception of the ecumenical movement in the Christian Churches is imperative if the credibility of the Churches, indeed Christianity itself, is to be maintained. 'Without reception there could be no authentic Christianity.'[16] This is not the place to attempt such a rationale with any depth or detail. I want to show only that this spirit of reception towards the modern ecumenical movement is rooted in faith, in Scripture and Tradition, in the recognition of a new developing relationship between historically separated Churches, in an ever expanding awareness of the demands of faith to live as one community of faith in rich diversity, aware of the action of the Holy Spirit, and with new theological resources for common reflection.

All this is not a gratuitous affirmation of the legitimacy of ecumenism in the life of the Church. It has its roots in the actual experience of a significant number of Christians active and faithful in all our Churches at many different levels of church life. It is also derived from certain principles for commitment and action.

These enable us to work for Church unity with integrity, in a spirit of patience and tolerance, 'speaking (and doing) the truth in love' (Eph 4:15). These basic principles respect conscientious convictions and the activity of the Holy Spirit in the whole Church through the ages. These are:

1. *Unity with legitimate diversity.* Differences in discipline, liturgy, spirituality and piety, cultural factors are not secondary factors in the search for unity. They are an integral part of the Church as catholic in its witness to the inexhaustible riches of Christ and the activity of the Holy Spirit. Unity comes from the unity of faith and the unity of doctrine which expresses faith.

2. *The development of doctrine.* In preaching the Gospel in every age and to every nation the Church grows in its understanding of the Gospel and the richness of God's revelation in Christ. Through the ages it expresses the Gospel in new and different ways.

3. *The hierarchy of truths.* This signifies a comparison of various teachings in historically separated Churches which have developed in this period of separation. These teachings are held in relation to an understanding of the foundational teachings of the Christian faith. They are received by other Churches as legitimate expressions of the faith-experience of those Churches as they contemplate the central mysteries of the Trinity and Incarnation, and an understanding of the workings of God's grace in Christ as well.

4. *The Church must be prepared for reformation and renewal always.* In every age the Church has to open itself for a review and examination of its fidelity to the Gospel and the gifts bestowed by the Holy Spirit for its life and mission.

5. *The Lund Principle.* This principle states that Churches ought to act together in all matters except those in which deep differences of conviction compel them to act separately.

6. *Ecumenism to be real has to be local.* This has reference to the daily life of local Churches and movements which involve the participation of significant numbers of pastors and lay people. It is the lived experience of ecumenism, the shared life of local congregations working for unity within the official disciplines of their denominations. It is in this more localized setting of the Churches that the Church is experienced *as a communion.* Here and now this communion is experienced as *imperfect.* Yet the desire for full communion with one another as Churches maintains the spirit of ecumenism in this place. At this level there can often be found an intimate sense of communion (*koinonia*), a deep commitment to ecumenism (*votum unitatis*), an active faith expressed in ecumenical co-operation and relationships (*sensus fidei*). In the local Church these technical terms are translated into the lived experience of the Church with a practical will for unity and an instinct that this is the true life of faith. Local ecumenism can inspire theologians and Church leaders to work at ecumenism more realistically. Perhaps this is what Cardinal Ratzinger meant when he said that local ecumenism 'is not just an executive organ of centralized top level ecumenism but rather an original form of ecumenism and an independent starting point for theological insights'.[17] This sixth principle along with the other five offers real hope for the ecumenical movement if adopted. Putting these principles to work ensures *reception* of ecumenism as a shared experience of the whole people of God of their oneness in Christ.

As we come to the end of our reflection on receiving the ecumencial movement in our Churches we may ask how this accords with the thought of John Henry Newman, some of whose thought was traced in the first three chapters. How would Newman receive the ecumenical movement of this century? Would he have been enthusiastic over the Decree on Ecumenism of Vatican II? Or would he reluctantly acknowledge it because of the official commitment of his Church to it?

There is no need to over-indulge our imagination to answer such questions. We have looked at significant areas of his thought in the course of his intellectual pilgrimage. It seems to me that these areas we have looked at suffice to guarantee the hypothesis that were he in our midst today his enthusiasm for the ecumenical movement would be energetic and unequivocal. In his time he wrote as apologist and polemicist, more as a philosopher of religion than a rigorous theologian. But his view of Tradition with its prophetic dimension and fidelity to Scripture would enable him to see that ecumenism is faithful to the past and the future. His position on the development of doctrine would enable him to see the continuity between an older vision of the Church as a communion of communions and the urgency to recapture this vision of the full communion of Churches envisaged by the ecumenical movement. His insistence on the active participation of the laity in bringing a sense of faith in doctrinal matters lends credence to the conjecture that he would subscribe to the participation of his Church in the ecumenical movement. His extraordinary spirit of faith in the Spirit's activity among all the members of the Church would alert him to the readiness of the laity to rediscover a deeper communion with their brother and sister Christians. He would test its spirit with intellectual and spiritual rigour. He would sense the irreversibility of the movement as Pope John Paul II spoke of it. Again he would respond to the Pope's description of Britain as 'privileged ecumenical terrain' with its special religious history of division and separation. As his spirit overshadowed the proceedings of Vatican II, so that same spirit offers us patronage and guidance on our pilgrim walk – hand in hand, speaking heart to heart – on our way to a renewed unity of faith and discipleship. Polemics and apologias have been converted to dialogue and convergence without shadow of compromising conscientiously held convictions. This would take place on that 'large mental field' of which Newman speaks in the very first chapter of his *Essay on the Development of Doctrine*. For him it would be 'a great idea... elicited and expanded by trial and battles into perfection and supremacy'. It seems appropriate to conclude with a text from Newman often quoted apart from its context. The full context is found in chapter one of the *Essay* where he is describing how 'a great idea' develops. If we think of such an idea as the ecumenical movement towards Christian unity his words seem apposite:

In time it enters upon strange territory; points of controversy alter their bearing; parties rise and fall around it; dangers and hopes appear in new relations; and old principles reappear under new forms. It changes with them in order to remain the same. In a higher world it is otherwise, but here below to live is to change, and to be perfect is to have changed often.

NOTES

1. *Ecumenical Trends*, vol. 18, n.10 (November 1989), p. 145.
2. Ibid. p. 156.
3. Ibid. p. 150.
4. For a deeper theological insight into the reception process see an article by Myroslaw Tataryn entitled: 'Karl Rahner and the Nature of Reception' in which he summarizes Rahner's approach to reception. Cf *One in Christ*, 1989-1, pp. 75-83.
5. J.M.R. Tillard, 'Reception: A Time to Beware of False Steps', *Ecumenical Trends*, vol. 14, no.10 (November 1985), p. 145.
6. Ibid. p. 146.
7. Ibid. p. 147.
8. Ibid. p. 145.
9. 'The Response of LCA to BEM', Faith & Order Paper III, adopted by the 1984 Convention of LCA. LCA is now part of the Evangelical Church in America with headquarters in Chicago, Illinois, USA, where there is an office for ecumenical affairs.
10. Lukas Vischer, 'The Process of "Reception" in the Ecumenical Movement', *Midstream*, 23 (1984), p.233.
11. This address was reprinted with permission in *Ecumenical Trends*, vol. 14, no. 3 (March 1985), pp. 38-47.
12. Cf the response to my article by Francis Fiorenza in *Ecumenical Trends*, vol. 15, no. 7 (July-August 1986), pp. 112-113.
13. Robert Butterworth, 'Reception and Pluriformity', *The Month*, 18 (1985), pp. 348-358.
14. J.M.R. Tillard, 'BEM: The Call for Judgment upon the Churches and the Ecumenical Movement', *Midstream* 23 (1984), pp. 234-250.
15. John Zizioulas, 'The Theological Problem of "Reception"', *Bulletin of the Centro Pro Unione*, 26 (1984), pp. 3-6; also published in *One in Christ*, 21 (1985), pp. 187-193; cf also Emmanuel Lanne, 'The Problem of Reception', *Ecumenism* 72 (1983), pp. 25-31; also 'The Report of the Third Forum on Bilateral Conversations' in *One in Christ*, 18 (1982), pp. 44-54.
16. Avery Dulles, 'The Reception Process in the Roman Catholic Church', a paper delivered at the Twenty-Second International Ecumenical Seminar in Strasbourg (2 July 1988).
17. Joseph Ratzinger. The full address of Ratzinger on local ecumenism may be found in the Information Service of the Secretariat for Promoting Christian Unity, no. 20, April 1973/11.

Chapter 6

The ordination of women

This chapter deals with a subject which is divisive within and among the Churches. The last chapter was about 'receiving ecumenism'. The issue of women's equality in secular affairs is often linked to the issue of women's ordination in the Churches. Such linkage may or may not prove helpful in the ultimate evolution of social consciousness over what is after all a matter of justice which can no longer be deferred – the complete recognition of the personal dignity and equality of women in human existence. However, the linkage is always helpful in clarifying theological issues surrounding women's ordination. In the ecumenical world it is considered by some Churches to be a serious obstacle to future Church unity. My purpose here is not to argue for or against the ordination of women. My purpose is a special pleading for all the Churches to consider this an open question, a discussable issue, even if at the present time it remains yet another Church dividing issue. And even though a particular Church has an official position in this matter of ordination, it ought to remain 'open' in ecumenical dialogue and within denominations. It would be presumptious to speculate on how John Henry Newman would have reacted had the question been raised in his time. But I do feel he would have considered it legitimate to form an opinion rooted in a theology of prophetic development arising out of a consensus of faith in the Church. With such a spirit of faith Christians need not be hesitant to search out the will of God in this respect.

In the ecumenical movement the overarching model for future Church unity is full communion or the *koinonia* of the New Testament.[1] Hence the question of women's ordination has become crucial in the search for full communion. For it is particularly divisive in that it touches life within and among the Churches. John Thornhill, a member of the Anglican-Roman Catholic International Commission (ARCIC), says that 'despite the vast volume of literature which has appeared, the debate leaves much to be clarified'. And he adds: 'Not only is there no clear consensus for or against the ordination of women, but a survey of this literature shows that there is no consensus as to the theological rationale which supports one or the other position.'[2] Consequently we are not dealing with the 'definitive' teaching of any Church, including Roman Catholic and Orthodox Churches. As the official Roman Catholic statement issued in 1976 says, 'we are dealing with a debate which classical theology scarcely touched upon'.[3] Nonetheless, arguments based on new and contemporary situations cannot bypass those of an earlier time. We have to pay attention to positions rooted in Tradition.

Tradition. Arguments from Tradition often proceed on the principle that there is no precedent. This lack of precedent in the matter of women's ordination to priesthood has then to be traced back to a theological rationale rooted in faith. This may be expressed as a matter of Christ's will for the Church or to the inherent symbolic function of eucharistic ministry, viz. that only the male person is a satisfactory icon of Christ's high-priestly ministry in human relations with God. I have referred previously to an understanding of Tradition which looks only to the past. It does not seem to take into account the principle of development in doctrinal matters for all practical purposes. John Henry Newman of course pioneered this theory of a 'development of doctrine' in such a way that it illustrates the living ongoing character of Tradition as a response of faith to Church growth and the fulfillment of the Church's prophetic ministry in the world. It is encouraging to hear a theologian describe the issue behind the problem of women's ordination in terms of a 'prophetic fidelity to the Church's tradition'.[4] For this very reason Thornhill advocates openness and further discussion. There is at stake an even more fundamental question, viz. 'how is the once-for-all truth of the tradition which lives in the Church to be interpreted within the context of a profound shift in cultural awareness?' Some would feel that we ought not pay much attention to the arguments from cultural awareness. For Orthodox theologians the Church stands over and above such cultural shifts in consciousness and society. It judges the secular world in its human history. It is not judged or conditioned by the socio-cultural order. Tradition is not subject to human actions and decisions – only to the Holy Spirit working in the councils of the Church. It helps to understand this Orthodox position if we remember that the Orthodox Church does not have a theology of dogmatic development nor a magisterium which speaks definitively on matters of faith and practice.[5]

There is of course an official position in the Roman Catholic Church. Since, however, no definitive decision has been made that Church remains open to the possibility that the present practice of ordaining only men could be changed in authentic fidelity to the

Tradition.[6] Canon Christopher Hill, also a member of ARCIC, says that 'Anglican provinces and individuals who have proceeded to the ordination of women have consistently stressed their action is a *development* of tradition, not a disjunction'. He quotes Archbishop Runcie making the point that if such a decision were to be made 'it must not be made on the basis of a change in the character of priesthood but as an expansion of eligibility to the priesthood'.[7]

Development. Such approaches make us return to the developmental view of Tradition. Of course there will remain notable differences in how we interpret development and Tradition. But where Tradition is understood as 'prophetic' and linked to the development of doctrine the norm of orthodoxy becomes both fidelity to the past and creativity for the future. Bishop John Baycroft, another Anglican member of ARCIC, argues that it is *exclusiveness* in the issue of women's ordination rather than *inclusiveness* that creates the problem for those working towards full communion of Churches as in the stated purpose of the ARCIC dialogue. He would say that it is the refusal to recognize or receive the ministry of ordained women that disturbs and disrupts the Anglican Communion and relations between Anglicans and Roman Catholics.[8] We will return to this pivotal concept of *koinonia*. For now, in the spirit of Newman, more has to be said about the linkage between Tradition and development. Then it is necessary also to look into the notion of the development of doctrine, or what Peter Chirico calls 'the dynamic aspects of revelation'.[9] I know of no one better suited to help in this task than Chirico.

When traditional theology speaks of revelation 'ending with the death of the last apostle' it does not mean that no new truth of revelation is possible. Chirico qualifies this by saying that what ceased with the death of the last apostle was the proclamation of the universal presence of the risen Christ by those who experienced it and had been associated with his ministry prior to his death. In this sense the primary witness to the Resurrection ceased for all time. What did not cease in any sense was the efficacy of the Resurrection itself. Since we are following Chirico closely in this matter it is best explained in his own words:

It continues to be the living object of universal revelation and, by its continuance, it generates the possibility of ever new facets of its intelligibility being grasped by men who encounter it in ever changing circumstances of life. Hence it is possible for the Church to pull out of its storehouse things both old and new. The Resurrection is an inexhaustible object of universal revelation; and as such it ultimately is a source of infallible teaching whose limits cannot be determined as long as time shall last and human development take place.[10]

It is this risen Christ who is open to all of creation in all its meanings. As humankind grows and development becomes more complex, 'Christ incorporates into his own humanity all that humankind achieves in an integral way'. Chirico continues:

This universal and unlimited growth process in Christ is paralleled by the growth processes in the Church that mark its development... They are discovered not at the very beginning of the Church's life but in the course of her history. In the attempt to live out the Gospel in a variety of circumstances the Church stumbles, falls, but invariably moves haltingly ahead. In the course of time she makes headway as a result of mistakes. As a very precipitate of that progress, she eventually is enabled to discern the recurring developmental patterns that mark her genuine growth.[11]

From this we can see that the development of doctrine is more than a theory. It comes out of high Christology, the Risen Universal Christ. It reflects the mystery of the Church, the whole Christ, head and members, vine and branches. It is a Christology which is likewise a Pneumatology, a theology which takes into account the ongoing activity of the Holy Spirit, sent from the Father through the Son to bring the Church into all truth and perfection. This takes place *in time* and it *takes time*. We are still stunned by the Resurrection. We stand at the edge of its universal meaning for all time and for all people. And as we make an effort in faith to grasp its meaning in bits and pieces as it were for ourselves and for others in the concrete circumstances of human life and growth, the Church formulates these meanings into specific doctrines expressed in dogmatic formulae from time to time.

Koinonia. The ecumenical movement has begun to renew in all the Churches a sense of identity, a sense of what it means to be the Church, a communion of communions. This notion of communion or *koinonia* between Churches has served in a notable way the dialogue between Anglicans and Roman Catholics. While the degree of communion between the two, indeed between all the separated Churches, is an imperfect communion which falls short of full communion, there exists between Anglicans and Roman Catholics a special relationship. Vatican II mentions

Anglicanism as holding 'a special place' because it is among those Communions 'in which some Catholic traditions and institutions continue to exist' (Decree on Ecumenism, c. 3, no. 13). One can infer the existence of important links between the two communions to warrant mentioning Anglicans by name. This special relationship has permeated ARCIC I and II, though ARCIC II has not completed its work to date. Both sides of the dialogue would agree that while all dialogue between the Churches is a quest for a renewal in faith and a deeper appropriation of a common tradition. ARCIC I 'carried that process forward in a remarkable way for both our communions'.[12] John Thornhill says that this happened because it took place within the Church's *koinonia* and ARCIC I's judgement that 'our two traditions are at one'.[13] This discovery of a common tradition in the midst of disagreements which persist over particular issues such as the ordination of women continues to be effective because of *koinonia.*

This communion between the two Churches arises from an abiding presence of God's truth in the Church, that under the grace of the Holy Spirit the truth of the Gospel can be articulated eventually *if we remain faithful to the common tradition.* Communion/*koinonia* is not an experience for a few people, albeit churchmen and theologians. To discover God's will and the requirements of the Gospel involves the whole community of faith – not least the lay members of that community. The danger in Churches taking unilateral decisions as a matter of course in this ecumenical period is that of further impairment of an already imperfect communion. Thornhill refers to the ARCIC I statement on authority (no. 8): 'In spite of diversities each local Church recognizes its own essential fea-

tures in the others and its true identity with them.'
Unilateralism in deciding major matters affecting the
common tradition will continue to be debated by the
Churches committed to ecumenism because such unilateral decisions, e.g. the ordination of women, necessarily makes an implicit judgement on the contrary
practice in other Communions.

The common tradition. Despite the danger to the
communion we are looking for in the ecumenical movement engendered by such unilateralism, we cannot
lose hope in our future communion. The more or less
imperfect communion already discovered between the
Churches is rooted in a common tradition. It is important to go on linking our sense of communion with our
sense of working from a common tradition. George
Tavard speaks of tradition as *'koinonia* in action'.[14] He
is making a point already stressed, viz. that in trans-
mitting the Gospel we are in a process of handing on.
This process is Tradition. As Tavard says, 'the process
of Tradition implies a "participation" in what the
whole Church does and in what other believers do.'[15]
He continues: 'In the process of Tradition the Church
becomes, shows itself to be, a community: all members share the same common life in the body of
Christ...'[16] When it comes to testing a particular doctrine or practice Tradition implies discernment on the
part of the Churches in their imperfect communion *as
Church.* Tavard suggests three norms for such discernment to take place. These are really norms for
discerning a genuine development of doctrine. While
Tavard acknowledges the seven norms offered by
Newman he offers the following which I only summarize here:

1. What is presented as the Gospel should be tested
by the faithful in relation to what they already live as

the Gospel, i.e. the testimony of the Holy Spirit in their hearts.

2. Account must be taken of historical continuity by past decisions and formulations of doctrine, and especially by biblical witness. All these become norms for further formulations of doctrine by those in authority in the *koinonia.*

3. The appeal to common experience is necessary in getting a reading of the signs of the times.[17]

As already indicated, the growth into full communion as Churches is a very slow process and its terrain very uneven. The process can be a source of impatience, indifference or discouragement. By relating *koinonia* to Tradition we come to understand that what is being developed is not necessarily for ourselves to be fully realized in our own time. Our present imperfect communion is always tending to a future which is not entirely conditioned by the past. Tradition is related to the virtue of hope. It exists, as Tavard says, 'for the sake of the transmission of the Gospel to future generations'.[18] This provides the development of doctrine with a real connection to Tradition. And both are related to the history of the Church including what has developed in the Churches in the years of separation and imperfect communion. For as Tavard says, Tradition developes as it 'passes through successive inculturations from age to age and from nation to nation'. It 'accumulates new experiences, adopts new formulae, acquires new aspects; it is humanly enriched by being expressed in more languages, received in more diverse backgrounds, correlated to various types of civilization'.[19] All this is a positive assurance that the common tradition is being enriched in our ecumenical age, this as the Church approximates what it is supposed to be – a communion of communions.

123

'Tradition looks forward, beyond history, to the full epiphany of the divine glory in the kingdom of God, and within history, to a more adequate imaging of the kingdom through a greater transparency of the Church to the *koinonia* of God with humanity.'[20] These words of Tavard summarize eloquently and precisely the value of our present ecumenical efforts to build communion in fidelity to a common tradition which has a past, a present and a future.

The diversion by way of stressing the relationship between Tradition and Church communion is necessary if we are to keep the question of women's ordination an open one for all the Churches; if we are to provide a rational, theological context for its reception or non-reception in a fully united Church. For if the question is to remain open, we must not prejudge the reception or non-reception of the ordination of women to priesthood and episcopacy. The Lambeth Conference of 1988 spoke a great deal about communion and tradition in terms of an ecclesiology of local and world-wide concerns. However, the Conference seemed to be absorbed by the need 'to hand on the new reality which is upon us', as P. Duprey, a Vatican observer at the Conference, put it. There was an extensive use of the 'reception factor' at the Conference in its deliberations on the ordination issue. It did weigh the danger of 'impaired communion' against receiving women's ordination. At Lambeth 'reception' came to mean an open process which is the work of the Holy Spirit. It would seem that part of the openness is 'living with the provisional' in such a way that it amounts to a kind of experimentation in the Church. For example, it was argued that the ordination of women priests in five provinces could be part of the reception process or non-reception of women bishops. There is a difficulty in this understanding of the reception process for some Churches. Roman Catholic and Orthodox Churches, perhaps some other Churches, do not view the reception process operating on such a loose, provisional, experimental basis. Rather, the process is a long conciliar consultative one in order to determine the sense of faith (*sensus fidei*) in this matter. The question of *how* reception works with the possibility of non-reception in this matter of new developments and praxis and how it will affect the communion of communions at which we aim 'will be with us well into the third millennium'.[21] Here and now we are expected to face the demands placed on us by the ecumenical question: Is the ordination of women in the catholic tradition of priesthood and episcopacy ruled out as incompatible with that tradition?

There is no substantive evidence of such ordinations in the early Church. The medieval Scholatics such as Aquinas, Bonaventure and Scotus raised this as a purely speculative question with the presumed negative reply worked out by different arguments. Such was the method of the Schoolmen in doing their theology. Today it seems like a 'setup'. It is only since the last century that the actual practice of ordaining women in Protestant Churches and in our own century in the Anglican Communion has lifted the question out of the purely speculative realm and made it a real question for all the Churches. Tavard would see the need for two levels of dialogue if the question is not to become hopelessly divisive for the Churches. At the first level he feels that the three traditions, viz. Protestant, Catholic and Orthodox 'should urgently enter into a series of dialogues on the proper foundation of Christian anthropology'. At the second level the dialogue on ministry must hold in balance and integrity its fourfold function of mediation (liturgy and sacraments), proclamation (word), service and education. He feels these would 'provide the starting point for an ecumenical theology of sacerdotal ministry and the substance of an eventual recognition of ministries'. He adds: 'It is also in this line that the question of the ordination of women ought to be fixed.'[23]

At the beginning of this chapter I said it was not my purpose to argue for or against the ordination of women. My purpose is to call attention to serious points of theology which may be helpful for contextualizing the dialogue over this ussue. If in reporting such areas for theological reflection one can feel a pull to one side or other of the question, this is all part of a discernment process. I purposely contrast dialogue and debate. There is more debate over the issue of women's ordination than dialogue. In the present climate arguments are presented with foregone conclusions. This is not entirely a bad thing, but it must be put in a wider interaction of dialogue which opens the Church to the discovery of God's will. To help with this progression from debate to dialogue the Klingenthal Report of 1979 is helpful. The official title of the Report is: 'Ordination of Women in Ecumenical Perspective'. The Report is one of three consultation-studies set up by the World Council of Churches. The other two are concerned with 'The Bible and the community of women and men in the church' and 'Towards a new theology of the human'.[24] While the report speaks of the continuing need for dialogue, it presents arguments on both sides of the question by way of a review. One line of argument proposes Tradition, as I have done, as flexible, subject to development and renewal, balanced between past and future, rooted in a sound doctrine of the Holy Spirit which acknowledges the action of the Spirit both in the Church and in the world at large. Only within such a view of Tradition can the goal of ecumenism, *koinonia*-communion be reconciled with a common Tradition.

Among the recommendations of the Report two are important for the purpose of this book. The first recommends 'that the Churches, within and among themselves, begin discussions on the issue of ordination of women'. The second recommendation is 'that the Churches, acknowledging this to be a *"burning issue"* now in the Church, pursue it seriously, with papers prepared for study by the Churches'. The Report itself gives six points for the dialogue to begin. I simply extract these points with the pertinent questions which must be asked and which must be faced together by those who wish to enter the dialogue.

1. *The new community of the Church*. Acknowledging that the nature of the Church is the essential starting point the Report asks: How does the way in which a Church tradition describes the nature of the Church affect its views of the possibility of women's ordination?

2. *The Church in ministries*. What is the significance of the variety of ministries in the New Testament... for the understanding of ministry and for the debate on the ordination of women to the ministry?

3. *Apostolic succession and tradition*. What is the relation of the understanding of apostolic succession and tradition to the understanding of ministry and to the question of the ordination of women?

4. *Incarnation and priesthood*. Is the maleness of the historical Jesus essential to the meaning of the Incarnation? Does Christ have to be represented by a male priesthood?

5. *The particular role of women in the Church*. Do

127

women have particular contributions to offer to the life of the Church which are different from or complementary to the contributions of men? Whatever the answer, does it have implications for the ordination of women?

6. *Personal vocation and true ministry of the Church.* What is the relation between personal vocation and the criteria for ministry applied by the Church?

At the end of this series of points for dialogue and the associated questions the Klingenthal Report offers a valuable comment. 'These six propositions, coming out of an ecumenical dialogue, both narrow and intensify the discussion. They are posed, not with the hope of agreement, but with the aim of discerning which issues are central and which are marginal to the work of achieving mutual understanding.'[25]

Particular points. Over and above providing a context for a proper ecumenical dialogue there are specific points which can clear the ground for a profitable discussion and discernment in the Churches over the next decade. Canon Christopher Hill raises one such point in a paper already mentioned.[26] We know that one of the objections to women's ordination is the harm it might do to the internal unity of a communion and the harm it may cause for ecumenical relations with other Churches. In the context of the Roman Catholic-Anglican dialogue (ARCIC II) Hill notes that this particular dialogue has not yet (1988) decided how to approach the ecumenical problem associated with such ordinations. One way suggested is to look at which is required for *koinonia*-communion. If, he argues, such ordinations were contrary to catholic faith, there could be no communion or even degrees of communion with Churches which so ordain. But if it is not a matter of faith or divine law, some degree of communion can be maintained despite anomalies. Such an approach would keep the dialogue going and the theological question open. He goes on to say that others in ARCIC II believe the Commission should treat the question directly and not simply see it as another sacramental divide between the two Communions. Regarding the reception or non-reception of women's ordination he says that the reception of change and development in the Church 'is necessarily slow and cannot be wholly identified with magisteriums and synods'. Again he says: 'Rome will need to recognize that this issue will not fade away. So also Anglicans who are opposed. Those in favour, Catholics and Anglicans, will also need the humility to recognize the development may be wrong. If it is a false step, it will wither. Reception is very much the Gamaliel principle: if a thing is of men (or women) it will fail, but if it is of God it will not be overthrown.'

Another point for serious consideration is the inclusive nature of the Church as sign of God's kingdom. The Church is by nature and purpose 'catholic' and as such intrinsically inclusive. Equal weight must be given to the ecumenical principle that the Church expresses its catholic nature through its *unity in diversity*. The principle can be used however to exclude women from priestly ministry in the catholic tradition. The argument states the view that being equal allows for difference and difference does not imply any status of subordination or inferiority, *but difference makes a difference*. Arguments against women's ordination use this as their point of departure. On the other hand the same principle of unity-in-diversity is used to argue that the absolute demands of God's kingdom do not favour diversity over inclusivity. So, we see that the arguments rooted in the essential witness the Church is called to give to the kingdom of God can be argued both ways. The two lines of argument are divided between what seems to be order and anthropological presuppositions in the Church and the absolute demands of a Gospel of the kingdom where reconciliation of differences, unity and communion characterize the children of God.

A final point to be made has been expressed by John Austin Baker when he says that 'the movement for the ordination of women has had to probe far deeper than mere reform of the institutional structures of the Church, and wrestle with fundamental matters of faith'.[27] He has an example in mind, viz. the theology of the Eucharist, 'which has developed without any reference to women or men as such'. Yet he objects to the fact that the question of who can confect the sacrament validly and licitly has been associated with a particular Catholic theology. What is presumed in such a theology is what Baker calls an 'iconic theory of the eucharistic presidency, confining the role to someone of the same gender as the Incarnate Lord...' To pursue such a theology is in Baker's opinion to run the risk 'of suggesting that Christ is present and active in the eucharistic minister in a unique mode and degree... for which there is no basis in the general doctrine of grace or in specific authoritative teaching'. Furthermore, he says, 'it blurs the nature of the Eucharist by presenting it as a re-enactment of the Last Supper, rather than fulfillment of the command there given to plead the sacrifice of the cross before God by the sacramental means proleptically provided.' He considers these 'serious distortions of Catholic belief.'[28] Baker asks if there is 'any theological reason why his [Christ's] action in the Eucharist should not take place through the agency of any duly ordained

130

and authorized member of the people of God, which as a whole "offers to God the Father the divine Victim in the sacrifice of the Mass" whether that member be man or woman?'. Here of course it is important to keep in mind the distinction between who represents and who is represented. Ministers of the Eucharist are *representatives* of Christ. They are not *representations* of Christ.

In making these particular points I do not wish to tip the scales unfairly in favour of the ordination of women. But as I indicated earlier one may feel the pull to one side or the other in the course of dialogue and reflection over the issue. This is inherent to the very nature of dialogue and reflection. After all it is the intrinsic worth of a particular argument that counts – not its appeal to unreasoned emotion. It remains an open question. My purpose is only to indicate some very solid foundations in ecumenical theology for further discernment by the Church as a whole, while the Churches together try to hear what the Spirit is saying to each and all of them.

NOTES

1. Cf my article in *Ecumenical Trends*, vol. 18, no. 1 (January 1989), entitled 'Koinonia as a Meta-Model for Future Church Unity', pp. 1-7.
2. John Thornhill, 'The Decision to Ordain Women and its Implications within the Context of Ecclesial Communion', *Clergy Review*, 72 (1987), pp. 57-65.
3. *Inter Insigniores* is a declaration of the Congregation for the Doctrine of the Faith of the Roman Catholic Church issued 15 October 1976. This statement is found in the introduction of the document.
4. Thornhill, op. cit., p. 60.
5. *Women and Priesthood*, ed. Thomas Hopko, Crestwood, NY: St Vladimir's Press, 1983. See also Kyriaki Fitzgerald, 'The Inter-Orthodox Theological Consultation on Women in the Church', *Ecumenical Trends*, vol. 18, no. 3 (March 1989), pp. 33-36. In the same issue of *E.T.* the text of the Inter-Orthodox Consultation is given. The Consultation was held between 30 October 1988 and 7 November 1988.

6. John Nilson, 'Let Bishops Give Proof of the Church's Motherly Concern: The Prospect of Women Bishops in Light of Vatican II', *Journal of Ecumenical Studies*, 25, 4 (Fall 1988), pp. 511-523. He looks at conciliar texts on the office of bishop, its nature and authority with regard to the ordination of women, concluding that Vatican II's theology of episcopacy does not *a priori* exclude women from this office. Of course it has to be understood that we need reasons *for* ordaining women as well as arguing that there are no reasons *against* such a practice.

7. *Women Priests?*, ed. Alyson Peberdy, Basingstoke, Hants, Marshall Pickering, 1988, p. 4.

8. John Baycroft, 'Inclusive Episcopacy and Koinonia', *One in Christ*, vol. 24, 1988/1, pp. 7-13.

9. Peter Chirico, *Infallibility: The Crossroads of Doctrine*, London: Sheed & Ward, 1977, pp. 176-179.

10. Ibid. p. 182.

11. Ibid. pp. 176-177.

12. Thornhill, op. cit. pp. 60-61.

13. Ibid.

14. George Tavard, 'Tradition as Koinonia in Historical Perspective', *One in Christ*, vol. 24, 1988/2, pp. 97-111.

15. Ibid. p. 104.

16. Ibid. p. 105.

17. Ibid. p. 108-109.

18 Ibid. p. 109.

19. Ibid.

20. Ibid. p. 110.

21. See my report in *Ecumenical Trends* on the Lambeth Conference of 1988, vol. 17, no. 40 (November 1988), pp. 145-148.

22. George Tavard, 'The Ordination of Women', *One in Christ*, vol. 23, 1987/3, pp. 200-211. Cf also John Hilary Martin, 'The Injustice of Not Ordaining Women: A Problem for Medieval Theologians', *Theological Studies*, 48 (June 1987), pp. 303-316.

24. *Ordination of Women in Ecumenical Perspective*, Faith & Order Paper 105, ed. Constance Parvey, Geneva: World Council of Churches, 1980. Extensive bibliography provided.

25. Ibid. p. 59.

26. *Women Priests?*, op. cit., pp. 1-11.

27. Ibid. p. 51ff.

28. If I understand him correctly such a statement would not conflict with the teaching of Vatican II on the special character of priesthood and episcopacy (cf Liturgy, 7, *Lumen Gentium* 21; *Christus Dominus*, *Presbyterorum Ordinis*, esp. 2 where it says: 'Therefore, while it indeed presupposes the sacraments of Christian initiation, the sacerdotal office of priests is conferred by that special sacrament through which priests, by the anointing of the Holy Spirit, are marked with a special character and are so configured to Christ the Priest that they can act in the person of Christ the Head.'

Chapter 7

Newman – A place in our time

In examining the theology of John Henry Newman in terms of three distinct phases of his life there is a kind of seedbed for a developing ecumenical theology in our time. In the earlier stage of his *Lectures on the Prophetical Office of the Church* (1837) and his correspondence with Abbé Jager (1834-1836) Newman was developing a sense and theology of Tradition. This theology would not deny the primacy of Scripture as a 'rule of faith'. It was an early attempt to establish a relationship between Scripture and Tradition. He began to think of Tradition in terms of developing insights into faith. Thus even in the early stage of his theology Tradition had a function whereby the Church could be oriented towards a future as a community of faith guided by its past. This aspect of Tradition would be further developed as Newman studied the Arian and Monophysite heresies.

Newman regarded the Church's role in society as prophetic. For him the entire Church is a teaching Church. Within its ranks are teachers who hand on and interpret the faith in new contexts and situations. Inspired by the Spirit they assist the whole Church in its discernment of present imperatives for its effective life and witness in the world. They enable the Church to walk in the newness of life promised in the Risen Christ (Rom 6:4). It is in this sense that Tradition in Newman's thought is always a prophetic Tradition.

This means that the Church lives in faith and fidelity to the revelation received in Christ while ever maturing in the understanding and practice and enrichment of the faith. The Church's character of catholicity enables this to be done in diverse ways which look to the whole and wholeness of human life.

This prophetic and catholic role can be realised only if the notion of development is taken seriously. In Newman's thought this is another way of saying that Christianity is an idea which is real and living. Christianity respects the role of reason and conscience as vital elements in the vigour of Christianity. By relating Scripture and Tradition, breathing into the latter a life of development and growth, while insisting on the proper role of reason and conscience in all this, Newman's theology provides a basic structure for the Church of today to continue its efforts in the restoration of visible Christian unity. This theology is the seed-bed for today's ecumenism.

Part of the ecumenical exercise is to reflect on what is essential in the very 'idea' of Christianity and church unity. Ecumenists reflect on a time prior to the major divisions within the Church. They reflect on the diversity of life and practice, the differences of doctrine engendered by the centuries of disunity. In the course of ecumenical relations and dialogue conscientious conviction enjoys the greatest respect and rational discourse the highest honour. In all this there is more than a will to 'patch up' differences and family quarrels. There is genuine hope that future church unity will be developed in such a way that the perfection of unity for which Jesus prayed (Jn 17) will be better realised in the future than in the past. This is the precise point where Newman's theology of a development of doctrine demonstrably works for the ecumenical dimen-

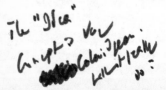

sion of Church life. The progress of ecumenism, however pedestrian it may seem, illustrates this. Keeping in mind the seven notes characteristic of true development which were treated in chapter two the modern ecumenical movement can be scrutinized for its authenticity and fidelity:

1. *The preservation of type.* Ecumenism is committed to search for what is essentially faithful and enriching in the 'idea' of Christianity. Whatever diversity there may be, there cannot be two Christianities. There is a diversity which is properly catholic and a diversity which is destructive of the unity in love prescribed by Jesus (Jn 13:34). Ecumenism begins with our oneness in Christ. The most basic model for Christian unity is that of *koinonia* or communion. These words are used to convey the intensity and intimacy of our union in Christ. This communion is of course a communion of persons, not simply as individuals, but as members of one community of faith. However, this *koinonia* type of communion is not to be treated as a disembodied relationship. It involves persons who even now live out the commandment of love, distinctly set out by Jesus to his followers, while living through the present tensions and differences which are a consequence of Christian denominationalism. This is a very special test of essential Christian love.

2. *Continuity of principles.* Ecumenism works with a set of principles out of which it ensures its own integrity. These were stated in chapter five. Over and above these each Church has its own set of principles which both allow it to participate in the ecumenical movement and at the same time manifest its own integrity and self-understanding *as Church*. By way of a familiar example the very first chapter of the Roman Catholic Decree on Ecumenism which came out of the

Second Vatican Council is entitled: 'Catholic principles of ecumenism'. There is only one ecumenical movement. Nonetheless, Churches in dialogue and relationships have to respect the various ways of church life, even the different ways in which these Churches may presently envisage Church unity. Any Church is entitled to state the principles from which it proceeds conscientiously to life in the ecumenical movement. Consequently there are principles shared by the Churches of the movement and there are principles which ensure denominational integrity. Both sets of principles are compatible, for ecumenism is a convergence process, a unity by stages, until we reach full communion, the unity Christ wills by the means he chooses. It is the commitment to such a convergence process which ensures a continuity of principles for the ecumenical movement.

3. *The power of assimilation.* One has only to look at the ecumenical movement in its history from 1910 onward to see how it accords with this test of development. No-one could rightly claim that it is an easy matter for Churches to take ecumenism into their ecclesial systems. The Churches have had to rely on the good will and spiritual vision of individual members in their Churches. More officially they have had to rely on instruments such as the World Council of Churches and other such councils – national, regional and local. Such official bodies, while indispensable, often substitute for a more intensive and intentional commitment on the part of Churches and church leaders. Obviously this will differ from place to place and according to circumstances. Yet they are part of the assimilative process as are other ecumenical projects. Still, all this is part of the assimilative process. Newman describes the phases of assimilation as polemical, then

seemingly eclectic, and finally truly uniting. Another way of putting it is to note that we have moved from extreme polemicism bred by the schism of East and West and those of the post-Reformation centuries to co-operative forms of ecumenism. From these many Churches have grown into a stage where co-operation becomes commitment to seek the unity Christ willed for the Church. This commitment expresses itself in forms of Church union or in a covenantal relationship which is an engagement rather than a marriage which is full communion. Ecumenism remains a movement with many dimensions of a doctrinal, spiritual and social nature. As an ongoing movement it illustrates the power of assimilation. Its power comes from the mission mandate given by Christ (Mt 28:18) and received by the Church. Its effectiveness stems from its fidelity to the mission entrusted to it by Christ and this effectiveness is in proportion to the unity of love and reconciliation to which it gives witness in its own life. Thus unity for mission provides the Church's power of taking ecumenism into the life of separated Churches.

4. *Logical sequence*. The ecumenical movement is not a planned, carefully contrived movement. It arose as a consequence of the International Missionary Conference at Edinburgh in 1910. It sprang from a sense of mission and a sense that this mission mandate to the Church was increasingly ineffective by multiple competing missionary church activities and preaching. The Church in its divisions had become an unworthy servant of the Gospel of Christ and something of a stumbling block to those to whom it has been carried by zealous Christian missionaries. These men and women began to ask ecclesiological questions: What is the Church for? What is the Church? How should the Church effectively bring its message of the good news

that we are truly reconciled in Christ. Such questions established a strong link between unity and mission.[1] Thus Christian Church unity was seen to be the answer to effective Christian mission, the latter being in logical sequence to the former.[2] And this Church unity is a logical sequence to our one baptism into Christ.

5. *Anticipation of a future*. It is the future that provides the dynamism for the ecumenical movement. It is a movement characterized as one of vision and hope. Such vision and hope carries a sense of responsibility and a sense of urgency to work for what we pray and hope for – the unity Christ wills for his Church 'that the world may believe' (Jn 17). It is this prayer of Christ and an impulse of the Spirit which gives ecumenists a feeling that unity is inevitable and the movement towards it irreversible. The future envisioned is neither purely utopian nor utterly eschatological. *It is a future in time.* Christian unity cannot be indefinitely postponed. Nor can the ecumenical movement be treated as an optional extra in the life of the denominations. We have not got all the time in the world to achieve a credible measure of Christian unity. We are pressed by the urgency to make God's word effective in the world. If ecumenism is at all eschatological, it is a *realised eschatology* wherein even now we experience a new, though always imperfect, degree of Christian unity. There is always the anticipation of the day when the Churches enjoy full communion among themselves.

6. *Conservation of the past*. The ecumenical movement has been careful to avoid giving the impression that its goal is to produce a super-Church, a Church which is an amalgam of presently divided Churches, a bionic frankensteinian Church. Such a notion is easily dispelled by a cursory reading of the Toronto State-

ment of 1950, a document received by the Central Committee of the World Council of Churches.[3] The World Council of Churches is not in the business of establishing a new Church. It aims to assist the Churches to rediscover and reintegrate into their common life and mission the unity bestowed and entrusted to the Church by Christ. It aims at helping the Churches reach a common confession of apostolic faith.[4] Conservation of the past does not mean the conservation of all that has come to be associated with the Churches in the course of their several histories. There is much theological, cultural and historical baggage to be left behind, to be discarded, even rejected insofar as it no longer conveys authentic Tradition nor serves the life, witness and mission of the Church. Newman would describe what today we call *renewal* as the conservation of the past which makes change 'real and perceptible, yet without loss or reversal of what was before... protective and confirmative of what went before'.[5] This is what the ecumenical movement and the World Council of Churches is all about.

7. *Chronic vigour.* The ecumenical movement is still young. It may be too early therefore to speak of its chronic vigour. Its ability to stand the test of time. There is widespread ignorance and indifference and not a little hostility towards it. It still lives under a cloud of suspicion among rank and file members of our Churches. There is little evidence that it enjoys high priority on church agendas. All this despite official commitment to it. Its reception by the Churches is something very much in its infancy. Yet it does claim official sanction and a measure of commitment by church leaders. Acknowledgement to be the will of Christ for the Church and the work of the Holy Spirit in the Church are the two factors which ecumenists

have in mind when they claim that the movement towards unity is irreversible or if we were to speak of it enjoying 'chronic vigour'.

Over and above these two factors there is official commitment. There is a core of theologians and ecumenists doing and communicating the theology of ecumenism. There is the structuring and restructuring of ecumenical instruments designed to promote ecumenism. There is the rise of organizations to promote Christian unity. And there is continuous cross-fertilization of many church activities along with a consistent pattern of prayer for such unity. These, together with a growing consensus that ecumenism is a work of the Spirit, seem to tip the scales in favour of 'chronic vigour'.

Ultimately the chronic vigour of ecumenism will be tested by the faith of the whole Church, i.e. by that sense of faith in the faithful we reflected on in chapter three where we dealt with Newman's approach *On Consulting the Faithful in Matters of Docrine*. We have described this as a sense of instinct found in all faithful members of the Church to choose the right path and direction for its faith and practice, though time is needed for a consensus in faith to be reached.

Education in the various principles governing the ecumenical movement is indispensable. Attitudes which prejudge the movement must be educated to a clear understanding of the aim and methods inherent in it. This is not to be confused solely with formal academic-theological education. There are various structures in our parishes and enough resource persons to ensure more informal opportunities for such ecumenical education. Such education is needed formally, especially in our seminaries and colleges of education.

It is equally necessary as part of ongoing adult education among clergy and laity. Only then can the 'chronic vigour' and consonance with Christian faith avowed by the ecumenical movement be truly tested. Ecumenism is a test of faith – faith in the presence of the Holy Spirit in the Church. Nor is it enough to grasp the principles of ecumenism intellectually. There is a spirituality in ecumenism which holds the vision of Christian unity before our minds and prepares our hearts, our attitudes, our emotions to receive this new thing that God is doing in our midst. Above all the movement towards Christian unity is always set against the horizon of Christ's will for his disciples in their mission to the world. This is the common vision ecumenists share however much they differ on the precise nature of the unity we seek for the Churches. The prayer of Christ (Jn 17) keeps the movement moving. Most certainly Newman would share this vision. Most likely he would feel comfortable with ecumenism as a process of development or convergence, unity by stages, one step at a time enough, the vision and the kindly light leading the Church to full communion.

In chapter four it was said that we have to take into account the internal problems and tensions within the denominations. These impinge on relationships with other Churches. It could be objected that for this reason I ought to have treated the divisive issue of authority and its exercise in our various Churches. I chose not to do this because this is already recognized as the basic problem in our continuing disunity and differences. It is also an internal problem for our Churches whatever their institutional structure, e.g. episcopal, papal, presbyteral, congregational, pentecostal. Differences within denominations surface over the *de facto* exercise of authority. These differences can siphon off our ecumenical energy and actually mislead ecumenical partners in dialogue or other forms of association.

I chose to address the issue of the ordination of women because it particularly highlights issues of authority and decision-making within and among our denominations. It seems to be an issue which will be with the Christian Churches for a long time. It most certainly will defer the full communion we seek among Christian Churches. It raises questions of ministry, its nature and function, for the Churches. And it raises once more an older question on the precise relationship between the ordained ministry in the Church vis-a-vis the ministry or priesthood of the faithful of all baptised members of the Church. It raises questions concerning Protestant, Anglican, Orthodox and Roman Catholic conceptions of ordained ministry. Many Churches insist on keeping distinct questions of what ordained ministry is and who may exercise it. Others see the what and who of such ministry much more closely associated. The issue also brings to the attention of the Churches some of the profound human implications and sensitivity experienced in our Churches over the ordination of women. These are not purely disciplinary matters. There are theological questions on the relationship of grace and nature, the sacred and secular in the life of the Church as sign and mystery of God's coming kingdom. The social question of the equality of men and women cannot be divorced entirely when the question of ordination is raised. Nor can it be entirely divorced from a time in history and in many societies when a new consciousness seems to be evolving over the equality and opportunity for women at every level of social and political life. Such questions do touch each other and are bound to be divisive. The ordination of women is yet another church dividing issue. As such it remains an open question theologically speaking. It is a legitimate ecumenical issue to be discussed by Churches who commit themselves to the ecumenical movement. It is an open ecumenical question – no more, no less. In this perspective its theological roots entail what we have reflected upon in the theology of John Henry Newman – tradition, development, consultation throughout the Church and between the Churches engaged in dialogue.

At any rate there is no evidence that this use will bring an end to ecumenical dialogue or relationships. While official Church positions demand respect all around, this does not mean that the theological spirit of further enquiry and openness need be diminished. Further enquiry and waiting upon the Spirit will either confirm certain theologies or bring us beyond them. Theological enquiry and an openness to receive what the Spirit is saying to the Churches can at very least lead to new considerations of the issue. Theology does not exist to undermine official positions. But if it is to serve the whole Church in its ecumenical endeavour, it cannot be denied this right to open enquiry in matters which as yet remain insufficiently examined and explored. The issue and question of women's ordination is an opportunity to test the crucial balance between theology and the teaching authority of the Churches. Such a balance was crucial in the life and to the mind of John Henry Newman. In pleading for openness to the issue of women's ordination at the theological level would seem to be faithful to his mind and spirit.[6]

Speaking from Newman's old pulpit in St Mary's, Oxford, on 6 March 1990, the centenary year of Newman's death, Archbishop Robert Runcie reflected on the ecumenical significance of Newman. His words seem apposite to close this final chapter:

> The coming together of the Churches after centuries of separation is not something which can happen overnight. Ideas and convictions are things which, as Newman saw, take time to mature and be realized. There is need for 'chronic familiarity'. The arresting phrase is his. Pope John Paul spoke recently in our conversation in Rome of the need for an affective collegiality to grow into effective collegiality. At many different levels, and in a multitude of ways, the broken unity needs to be slowly restored, the underlying continuity recovered. In this process the person and teaching of Newman has a special place.[7]

NOTES

1. Cf Emmanuel Sullivan, *Baptized into Hope*, SPCK, London, 1980 pp. 33-59.
2. Barry Till describes the World Council of Churches as 'the institutional response of the institutional Western Churches to their conscience about their disunity'. *The Churches Search for Unity*, Penguin Books, 1972, p. 289.
3. The Toronto Statement of 1950 is entitled: 'The Ecclesiological Significance of the World Council of Churches'. Note especially section III: What the World Council of Churches is Not.
4. Cf Hans-Georg Link, ed. *One God, One Lord, One Spirit: An Explication of the Apostolic Faith Today*, WCC, Geneva, 1988. Also Hans-Georg Link, *The Roots of Our Common Faith: Faith in the Early Church*, WCC (Faith and Order Paper 119), Geneva, 1984. Also by Hans-Georg Link, *Apostolic Faith Today: A Handbook for Study*, WCC (Faith and Order Paper 124), Geneva, 1985.
5. See *The Development of Doctrine*, the introduction to chapter 11.
6. Newman sought to redress the imbalance both in his 1877 Preface to the *Lectures on the Prophetical Office of the Church* and in his *Apologia* where he discusses his position and thinking since 1845.
7. *Newman: A Man for Our Time*, ed. David Brown, SPCK, London, 1990. 'An Ecumenical Perspective', a centenary sermon by Robert Runcie, p. 165.

Epilogue

It has not been an easy pilgrimage for the Church, or
the world for that matter, in the journey from the
nineteenth century to the twentieth. It promises to be
no easier, perhaps more difficult, as we prepare for the
third millennium of Christian history in the final decade of this century. Early in the century Nicholas
Berdyaev was writing about 'the end of our time' in
terms of what was happening in Russia and in Europe.
For him the old world, his expression for the modern
age, was at an end. Indeed he speaks of a 'decomposi-
tion' of that world and the coming to birth of a new
and unknown world. Over two decades ago Alvin
Toffler wrote *Future Shock* which he memorably defined as a 'dizzying disorientation brought on by the
premature arrival of the future'. He followed this with
The Third Wave, an image of the electronic age which
follows upon the agricultural and industrial ages. These
works are remarkably prophetic when reread in our
present time. They belong more to the prophetic literary genre than that of the political-sociological kind. I
am aware of false prophecy in its modern disguises –
gratuitous assumptions based on manipulated statis-
tics, guessing about the future, naive optimism or
apocalyptic pessimism splashed from a thinktank, a
kind of science fiction. Helpful as these may be in a
proper context, they lack the confirmation of experience which announces some measure of fulfillment –
even now, but not yet. The perception of Berdyaev or
Toffler echo the cry of the ancient prophet: 'Behold, I

am doing a new thing; now it springs forth, do you not perceive it? I will make a way in the wilderness and rivers in the desert' (Is 43:19). The Judaeo-Christian experience has always been one of tension between the old and the new, the past and the future. Some periods of human history experience this tension in the extreme. It seems ours is such a period.

What I am suggesting in these pages may seem unreal, at first reading. I am suggesting that the intellectual development of a remarkable nineteenth century man whose changing thought mismatched the relative stability of his Victorian times could be fruitful for our own fast-moving ones. Life in the Church needs his vision and wisdom and holiness to make this passage from another old world to another new one. In his recent book, *A New Vision of Reality*, Dom Bede Griffiths powerfully persuades us of one formidable task – to integrate Western science, Eastern mysticism and Christian faith. What is immediately needed is a sense that something quite new is taking place. We are being asked as a people of God to test the spirits of our age – not in terms of technology alone, nor in the formation of instant opinion, but in terms of a growing collective consciousness, in terms of the uneven currents of human life, in terms of solid doctrine and theological discourse. We need to ask where these currents are taking us. We need not ask to see the distant scene, but to take those few steps, perhaps only one step which will be enough for us to be led as was John Henry Newman by the power of God's Spirit over moor and fen, crag and torrent, until the night is gone and a new age dawns. Another poet, T.S. Eliot, captured the spirit of Newman in wanting the past, present and future to hold together when he wrote:

We shall not cease from exploration
And the end of all our exploring
Will be to arrive where we started
And know the place for the first time.

This is the best kind of
'open' Catholicism.
I yield to no one in admiration of
much of what Newman wrote but —
as with Wesley — he was a
man of his age: a) cannot help
he wasn't to determine our
policy much as we can
learn from him.

147

Selected Readings

Newman

Owen Chadwick, *From Bossuet to Newman*, Cambridge University Press, 1957.

Charles Stephen Dessain, *John Henry Newman*, Thomas Nelson & Sons Ltd, 1966.

Sheridan Gilley, *Newman and His Age*, London: Darton, Longman & Todd, 1990.

Ian Ker, *John Henry Newman: A Biography*, Oxford: Clarendon Press, 1988. This biography has been described as an intellectual and literary biography.

Ian Ker, *The Genius of John Henry Newman: Selections from his Writings*, Oxford: Clarendon Press, 1989. This selection by Ian Ker presents a portrait of Newman as educator, philosopher, preacher, theologian and writer. Each section has a helpful introduction by Ker.

Ian Ker, *The Achievement of John Henry Newman*, London: Collins, 1990.

Nicholas Lash, *Newman on Development*, Sheed & Ward, 1975.

Newman After A Hundred Years, ed. Ian Ker & Alan G. Hill, Oxford: Clarendon Press, 1990.

Ecumenism

Robert McAfee Brown, *The Ecumenical Revolution: An Interpretation of the Catholic-Protestant Dialogue*, Burns & Oates, 1967. There is a text provided in the Appendix of the Vatican II Decree on Ecumenism (21 November 1964). In this work there is also an extensive bibliography on ecumenism.

Yves Congar, *Diversity and Communion*, SCM Press, 1984. Also published by Twenty-Third Publications, Mystic, CT.

The Decree on Ecumenism *(Unitatis Redintegratio)*. This is the official statement and commitment of the Roman Catholic Church to the ecumenical movement.

Paul Minus, *The Catholic Rediscovery of Protestantism: A History of Roman Catholic ecumencial pioneering*, New York: Paulist Press, 1976.

William Rush, *Reception: An Ecumenical Opportunity*, Fortress Press, 1988.

Barry Till, *The Churches Search for Unity*, Penguin Books, 1972.

Ordination of women

Women Priests: Obstacle to Unity? This publication of the Catholic Truth Society (DO 576) contains the official Roman Catholic Declaration and Commentary from the Congregation for the Doctrine of the Faith. It also has correspondence on this subject between Archbishops Coggan and Runcie and Pope Paul VI; also correspondence between Archishop Runcie and Pope John Paul II; also correspondence between Cardinal Willebrands and Archbishop Runcie.

Manfred Hauke, *Women in the Priesthood: A Systematic Analysis in the Light of Creation and Redemption*, Ignatius Press, 1989.

Thomas Hopko, ed., *Women and Priesthood*, St Vladimir's Press, 1983.

Constance Parvey, ed., *Ordination of Women in Ecumenical Perspecitve*, Faith & Order Paper 105, World Council of Churches, 1980. Bibliography of literature on the subject from 1960-1980 is provided.

Alyson Perbedy, ed., *Women Priests?* Marshall Pickering, 1988.

Appendix

Sermon by the Reverend Dr John A. Newton,
Free Church President of
Churches Together in England

A Celebration
St Paul's Cathedral, Friday 23 November 1990

'And he said to them, "Therefore every scribe who has been trained for the kingdom of heaven is like a householder who brings out of his treasure what is new and what is old"' (Mt 13:52).

John Henry Newman might, or might not be, astonished at today's celebration. At one level no doubt he would. Edward King, an Anglican contemporary and admirer of Newman, has a sermon on 'The surprise of the saints', in which he claims, 'Most of us ordinary people know how to be a great deal better than we are, but really good people are generally a great deal better than they know how to be; they are not conscious at all of being what they are. They are simply what they are, good people, and so they are surprised when the result of their lives at all comes out into view.'

Newman might well have shared that surprise. On the other hand, he had a most lively sense of what it is to live in time. He knew the whole world, physical and human, to be in process and development. 'To live is to change, and to be perfect is to have changed often', was his watchword. He learned to be patient, to take

153

the long view, believing that, 'Time will set a great many things right, and time only.' So perhaps he would not have been astonished today to hear the choirs of Westminster Cathedral and St Paul's blending their voices, or to see this great gathering from across the Churches, and from the City of London in which he was born. As early as 1841, he could look forward to Anglican-Roman Catholic unity, *'in God's time,* though, it may be, not in our day.'

What would surely have amazed him, would be the special cause of our gratitude to God, namely, the gift of his servant, John Henry Newman himself. Yet he always had a most lively sense of the creative individual acting in history. He looked to persons, rather than committees, to get things done. He was just such a creative individual himself, 'a scribe trained for the kingdom of heaven... who brings out of his treasure what is new and what is old.'

The Christian scribe

St Matthew is speaking here of the Christian teacher. To call him a scribe is to root him in the rich Jewish soil from which Jesus and the Gospel sprang. To describe him as 'trained for the kingdom of heaven' is to link him on to the new thing that God has done in Christ. Newman, as a Christian teacher, brought out of his treasure things old and new, which still enrich the Church and the world.

'To live is to change', he tells us; and he certainly exemplified that truth. He was in turn: an Evangelical Anglican, a Liberal, a Tractarian High Churchman, a Roman Catholic. Yet there is extraordinary continuity and coherence in his spiritual development. The changes he made were never easy, and often agonizing. But he sought to be obedient to the truth, and to follow the leading of the Spirit. He was a loyal son of both the Church of his birth, and the Church of his later allegiance. He made no wholesale repudiation of his Oxford Anglicanism. When as a Roman Catholic he republished his Anglican sermons, he neither changed their text nor altered their meaning by editorial additions. His catholicity would not allow him to do so. Yet, in the end, his quest for truth and holiness led him indubitably to Rome.

What is old

That same amplitude of view he brought to his work as a Christian 'scribe'. He drew from his treasure, first, what was old. He went to the roots of the Christian tradition, in the Scriptures and the early Fathers of the Church. His Oxford friend, Tom Mozley, records that he had an 'immense and almost minutely reverential knowledge of Scripture'. From Scripture he went to the Fathers, who took him behind the later divisions of Protestant, Catholic and Orthodox, to the formative period of Christian history, when diversity in unity was substantially a fact. In the Scriptures and the Fathers also, he rediscovered the doctrine of the 'indwelling' of the Holy Spirit, which gives life and power to religion. Grasp of this truth enabled him to make a profound contribution to ecumenical theology in his *Lectures on Justification* (1838). He broke through the often sterile controversy about faith and works, to see that justification, being made right with God, is the gift of the indwelling Spirit, who bestows both faith and renewal as his fruits. It was not a matter of playing off faith and good works against each other. Rather, in the words of St Paul, the heart of the matter was, 'faith, working through love' (Gal 5:6).

What is new

Newman brought out of his treasure not only what is old, but also what is new. He never sought for novelty in religion. What he did was to explore the inexhaustible riches of Christ, in the Gospel and the Church. Yet he did it, not in a cloister of the mind, but in ardent dialogue with the thought of his age. F.W.H. Myers could write of the 1870s, when scepticism was seeping through Newman's Oxford, 'This was the very flood-tide of Materialism and Agnosticism – the mechanical theory of the universe, the reduction of all spiritual facts to physiological phenomena. It was a time when, not the intellect only, but the moral ideas of men seemed to have passed into the camp of negation'. Like St Philip Neri, his patron, Newman had, 'a sympathy with the new spirit of the age and a desire to use the best of it for God'.

He was not like Christopher Wordsworth, the learned Anglican Bishop of Lincoln, who, as was said, 'had one foot in heaven and the other in the third century'. Newman was rooted in his own tumultuous age, alive to its questionings, even anticipating some of its central ideas. Mark Pattison, writing over thirty years after Newman's *Essay on the Development of Christian Doctrine* (1845), saw it as anticipating Darwin's evolutionary thought. 'Is it not a remarkable thing', he wrote, 'that you should have first started the idea – and the word Development – as the key to the history of Church doctrine: and since then it has gradually become the dominant idea of all history, biology, physics, and in short has metamorphosed our view of every science and of all knowledge.'

Newman had no difficulty with Darwin's evolutionary theory, because he already understood all life in time as change, process and development. But for him it was no blind, aimless process. It was purposeful, shaped by the Creator Spirit himself. It meant intensely, and meant good. The view that the universe in all its parts is intelligible, but in sum total is irrational and without meaning, Newman found frankly incredible.

Yet Newman took Darwin very seriously. He saw that if it is true that 'to live is to change', that must apply to the Church too. It must be true to the revelation given in Jesus Christ, and yet adaptable in life and message to the challenge of each new age. In the language of the Second Vatican Council which some have called Newman's Council, the Church needs *aggiornamento*, adaptation to new circumstances, as these are shaped by the Lord of history. Newman would have agreed with W.R. Inge, sometime Dean of this cathedral, that the Church which marries the spirit of the age is left a widow in the next generation. Newman was for critical engagement with the new age exposing its weaknesses in the light of the Gospel, and responding to its fresh insights into truth.

Finally, among 'what is new' in Newman's treasure, we should include his longing for unity and renewal in the Church of God. He anticipates the spirit of the Second Vatican Council when he regrets the scorn with which some Catholics 'treat proceedings and works among Protestants which it is but Christian charity to ascribe to the influence of divine grace'. He would surely rejoice at the immense increase in Christian charity between Catholics and Protestants in our day. At the same time, he would certainly remind us, as we tread the path to fuller unity as Pilgrims Together, that any unity worthy of the name of Christ must be unity in holiness and unity in truth.

So then, let us with one mind and one mouth thank God for his servant, John Henry Newman, pastor, prophet, witness to the truth, defender of the faith. His own Church has yet to decide whether formally to acknowledge him as saint and Doctor of the Church. Yet, whether canonized or not, he surely bears the marks of goodness and holiness, longsuffering and integrity. Since his death, as in his lifetime, he has drawn many hearts and minds to the truth as it is in Jesus. He himself confessed, 'I have nothing of the saint about me... It is enough for me to black the saints' shoes – if St Philip uses blacking in heaven'. Yet that sense of unworthiness, far from disqualifying him, may serve only to remind us, in the words of Austin Farrer, that,

> Saints are not men who store goodness in themselves, they are just men who do not delay to repent, and whose repentances are honourable. The saints have tired God's patience to the utmost, they have explored illimitable mercy; they have found that, through and through and up into the height of heaven, God's terror is the very flame, love burning in a blessed society of equal person, Father, Son, and Holy Ghost.

And now, to that Trinity of the Divine Love, who gave us John Henry Newman, and who in Jesus gives us all things richly to enjoy, be praise and glory, thanksgiving and power, for ever and ever. Amen.